U0483728

符号中国 SIGNS OF CHINA

中国瑞兽祥禽

AUSPICIOUS ANIMALS AND BIRDS IN CHINESE CULTURE

"符号中国"编写组 ◎ 编著

中央民族大学出版社
China Minzu University Press

图书在版编目(CIP)数据

中国瑞兽祥禽：汉文、英文 /"符号中国"编写组编著. —北京：中央民族大学出版社，2024.8
（符号中国）
ISBN 978-7-5660-2324-7

Ⅰ.①中… Ⅱ.①符… Ⅲ.①图腾—民族文化—介绍—中国—汉、英 Ⅳ.①B933

中国国家版本馆CIP数据核字（2024）第017474号

符号中国：中国瑞兽祥禽 AUSPICIOUS ANIMALS AND BIRDS IN CHINESE CULTURE

编　　著	"符号中国"编写组
策划编辑	沙　平
责任编辑	陈　琳
英文指导	李瑞清
英文编辑	邱　械
美术编辑	曹　娜　郑亚超　洪　涛
出版发行	中央民族大学出版社
	北京市海淀区中关村南大街27号　邮编：100081
	电话：（010）68472815（发行部）　传真：（010）68933757（发行部）
	（010）68932218（总编室）　　　　（010）68932447（办公室）
经 销 者	全国各地新华书店
印 刷 厂	北京兴星伟业印刷有限公司
开　　本	787 mm×1092 mm　1/16　印张：9.25
字　　数	128千字
版　　次	2024年8月第1版　2024年8月第1次印刷
书　　号	ISBN 978-7-5660-2324-7
定　　价	58.00元

版权所有　侵权必究

"符号中国"丛书编委会

唐兰东　巴哈提　杨国华　孟靖朝　赵秀琴

本册编写者

秦　芮

前言 Preface

　　"瑞兽"和"祥禽"指的是中国传统文化中具有吉祥寓意的动物。这些动物承载着深厚的历史文化内涵，蕴含着丰富的审美心理和民俗观念，是古时候人们祭奠祖先和"神灵"，祈盼繁衍、驱灾、避祸的吉祥物。人们通过赋予这些动物不同的寓意，表达了对美好事物和幸福生活的向往和追求。

Auspicious animals and birds refer to creatures that symbolize propitiousness in traditional Chinese culture. These animals have profound historical and cultural connotations, representing ancient Chinese aesthetic criteria and folk customs. They have been used in ritual ceremonies for ancestors and gods, as well as praying for procreation and expelling calamity in ancient times. Although each animal embodies different meanings, they all have expressed people's pursuit of good things and happiness in life.

Accompanied by exquisite pictures, this book introduces how auspicious animals and birds have developed in major historical periods and what they symbolize. Readers can gain a further understanding of the propitious connotations of these animals and traditional Chinese culture, through this book.

本书讲述了瑞兽、祥禽的文化内涵在各个历史时期的发展进程，着重介绍了这些动物具有的吉祥含义，并且配以精美的插图，读者可通过本书对瑞兽、祥禽这一中国吉祥文化的重要表现形式有所了解，并由此进一步了解中国传统文化。

目录 Contents

瑞兽和祥禽的源流
Origin of Auspicious Animals and Birds 001

原始图腾崇拜
Primitive Totemism 002

祥瑞文化的发展和兴盛
Development and Prosperity of
Auspice Culture 005

瑞兽
Auspicious Animals 011

华夏图腾——龙
China's Totem: Loong 012

仁德高贵——麒麟
Noble Spirit: Kylin 026

镇宅驱邪——虎
Home-guarding Exorcist: Tiger 030

百兽之王——狮
King of All Animals: Lion 033

勇猛矫捷——豹
Agile Warrior: Leopard 037

太平安定——象
Peace and Tranquility: Elephant 039

瑶光清明——鹿
Holy and Pure: Deer 043

昌盛发达——马
Prosperous and Flourishing: Horse 046

任劳任怨——牛
Industriousness and Gentleness: Ox 052

仁义吉祥——羊
Benevolence and Auspiciousness: Sheep 057

殷实有福——猪
Be Well-off and Blissful: Pig 062

玉兔呈祥——兔
Nimble Gentle as White as Jade: Rabbit 067

封侯晋爵——猴
Promoting to Nobility: Monkey 071

千岁而灵——龟
Immortal of Longevity: Tortoise 076

飞鼠迎福——蝙蝠
Flying Elf of Felicity: Bat 080

祥禽
Auspicious Birds 085

四海升平——凤凰
The Whole World Is at Peace: Phoenix 086

仙游长寿——鹤
Traveling Immortal with Long Life: Crane 092

富贵有情——孔雀
Fortune and Affection: Peacock 097

恩爱忠贞——鸳鸯
Love and Loyalty: Mandarin Duck 101

恋家报春——燕子
Homelover and Spring Herald: Swallow 104

灵禽兆喜——喜鹊
Sacred Bird Predicting Happiness: Magpie 108

鸟中君子——鸡
Gentleman among Birds: Rooster 113

安居乐业——鹌鹑
Stable Settle-down and Content Job: Quail ... 118

夫妻偕老——白头翁
Live to Old Age in Conjugal
Bliss: Chinese Bulbul 120

长寿富贵——绶带鸟
Longevity and Fortune: Paradise Flycatcher ... 122

优雅自由——鹭鸶
Elegance and Freedom: Egret 125

仁德守信——大雁
Kindness and Trustworthing: Wild Goose 129

瑞兽和祥禽的源流
Origin of Auspicious Animals and Birds

中国古代有"天人感应""万物有灵"之说。古人认为上天是有感情的，时刻关注着世间的万物，即"天人感应"；而世间万物是有灵性的，动物和植物都具有某种与上天和人类沟通的能力，即"万物有灵"。于是，中国的传统文化中就出现了瑞兽、祥禽这一文化现象。人们将这些祥瑞动物应用于建筑、服装、书画、器具的装饰上，希望以此来保佑自己平安、吉祥、幸福。

Ancient Chinese believed in the interaction between heaven and man that the universe emotionally connects with and watches attentively all natural things; they also believed in animism that all things such as plants and animals have spirits and can communicate with the universe and human beings. Therefore, auspicious animals and birds play an important role in traditional Chinese culture. Pictures and symbols of these animals can be found on the decoration of buildings, clothes, books, paintings, vessels and utensils as a blessing for safety, luck and happiness.

> 原始图腾崇拜

上古时期的先民尽管饱受着凶禽、猛兽的威胁和侵害，却又常从它们身上获得较多的益处，因而以既畏惧又渴望的矛盾心态对待它们，并将它们视为"灵物"加以崇拜。这可能就是各种与动物相关的传统及信仰的来源。

处于氏族社会的原始人，往往认为自己的祖先来源于某种动物或植

> Primitive Totemism

In ancient times, people suffered from the threat and encroachment of fierce animals and birds, but they benefited from them as well. Therefore, they had ambivalent feelings towards them and worshiped them. Perhaps, this is the reason why legends and beliefs about mysterious creatures were born.

Primitive people believed that their ancestors were from certain animals or

- 人面鱼纹彩陶盆（新石器时代）

出土于陕西半坡遗址，盆内壁以黑彩绘出两组对称的人面鱼纹。古代半坡人在很多陶盆上画有鱼纹和网纹图案，表达期盼富足的美好愿望。

Colored Pottery Basin with Face and Fish Patterns (The Neolithic Age, approx. 8000 years ago)

This basin was unearthed from relics of Banpo Culture in Shaanxi Province. Its inside was painted with two sets of symmetrical faces and fish patterns. Most basins from the Banpo Culture have fish and net patterns, which represent Banpo people's hope for affluence.

蛇形纹双耳陶壶（新石器时代）
Pottery Ewer with Snake Patterns (The Neolithic Age, approx. 8000 years ago)

物，或是与某种动物或植物有亲缘关系，于是便将之当作本氏族的标志或名号，这就是图腾崇拜。在中国的原始图腾崇拜中，对动物的崇拜占大多数。原始社会时，在我国的东南沿海一带，许多部落以鸟为图腾；而中原一带的部族多以两栖动物或鱼类为图腾；西北高原一带的部族则多以野兽为图腾。从发展过程来看，图腾经过了一个由单一至综合的演化过程。最早的图腾形象往往是蛇、鹤、熊等单一的动物，后来逐渐成为一种综合了多种动物特点的幻想中的"神兽"。例如，龙兼有蛇、兽、鱼等多种动物

plant or they were close relatives of these animals or plants. Thus, they regarded them as symbols or names for their tribes, starting the primitive totem worship. Animals were more likely to be used as totems. For example, primitive societies along the southeast coast of China made birds as their totems; in central China, however, most totems were amphibians or fish, whereas in northwest plateau's tribes, beasts were the major type of totems. Totem worship has gone through an evolutionary development process, starting from real animal worship, like snake, crane or bear, to integrated supernatural beings that combine the characteristics of a variety of animals, such as loong having the shapes of snake, beast and fish, and phoenix owning

龙纹玉璜（西周）
Semi-annular Jade *Huang* with the Loong Pattern (Western Zhou Dynasty, 1046 B.C.-771 B.C.)

• 鸟形玉雕（商）
Bird-shaped Jade Carving (Shang Dynasty, 1600 B.C.-1046 B.C.)

• 青玉虎形佩（春秋）
Tiger-shaped Green Jade Pendant (Spring and Autumn Period, 770 B.C.-476 B.C.)

的形态，凤兼有鹰、孔雀等多种鸟的特征，等等。

先秦诗歌总集《诗经》中有"天命玄鸟，降而生商"的诗句。传说商代的始祖契由他母亲简狄吞下鸟卵而生，因此，商王朝对鸟十分尊崇。

features of eagle, peacock and other birds.

According to the verse "A mysterious bird gives birth to Shang" in *The Book of Songs* written in the Pre-Qin Period (before 221 B.C.), Xie, the ancestor of the Shang Dynasty (1600 B.C.-1046 B.C.) was born after his mother Jiandi swallowed a bird egg. Therefore, bird worship was popular during the Shang Dynasty.

> 祥瑞文化的发展和兴盛

两汉时期，瑞兽、祥禽崇拜盛行。汉代的画像石上，就有诸多龙、鹿、虎、鱼等"仙鸟"和"神兽"的形象。

• 《五瑞图》拓片
Rubbings from the Five Auspicious Painting

> Development and Prosperity of Auspice Culture

During the Han Dynasty (206 B.C.-220 A.D.), the worship of auspicious animals and birds prevailed. On the stone relievo carved in the Han Dynasty, there are many images of auspicious animals, including loong, deer, tiger, bird and fish.

The most ancient extant auspicious pattern was the *Five Auspicious Painting* on the precipice that is located in Fengquan Gorge of Chengxian County in Gansu Province, which was created in the fourth year of Emperor Ling's reign (171) of the Eastern Han Dynasty (25-220). This painting is famous for its illustration of five auspicious patterns, including a yellow loong, a white deer, a double-trunk tree, the nectar and a magic crop seedling. On the left side of the

人首蛇身"神"，象征人类的始祖
The god with human head and snake body symblizes the ancestor of humans.

月亮，上有蟾蜍和玉兔
On the moon, there is a toad and a rabbit.

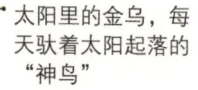

太阳里的金乌，每天驮着太阳起落的"神鸟"
The golden crow in the sun is a mythical bird that lifts the sun every day.

拄杖而立的老妇，即墓主人辛追夫人
The old lady with a cane is Xin Zhui, the owner of the tomb.

天门，由神豹和门神把守
Magical leopards and door gods guard the gate of heaven.

举行祭祀仪式的亡者家人
Her family at her funeral are included.

传说中的"地神"鲧，托举着大地，脚踩两条鳌鱼
Gun (a magical fish in legend) is holding the land and standing on two giant codfish.

- **湖南马王堆汉墓出土的"T"形帛画（西汉）**

  这幅帛画的内容分为上、中、下三部分，分别描绘了"天界"、人间和"地狱"景象。整个画面构图复杂，内容繁复，刻画细腻，色彩绚丽，天、地融为一体，人、"神"相安共处。

  T-shaped Silk Painting Unearthed from Mawangdui Tomb of the Han Dynasty in Hunan Province (Western Han Dynasty, 206 B.C.-25 A.D.)

  The painting includes three sections that reveal how Heaven, Earth and Hell look like respectively. The picture has complicated composition, including complex content, refined lines and marvelous colors, expressing how harmoniously and peacefully the humans and gods could coexist.

中国现存最早的吉祥图案是东汉灵帝建宁四年（171年）的摩崖石刻《五瑞图》，位于甘肃成县城西的丰泉峡中。此图因描绘了黄龙、白鹿、连理树、甘露、嘉禾五种祥瑞图案而得名。画中左面是黄龙，右面是白鹿；画的下方左面是两株连理树，右面一棵树下有一人，手中托着盘子接甘露，树的中间有一棵"一茎九穗"的禾苗。

魏晋南北朝时期，祥瑞文化进一步发展，吉祥物开始形成了一些固定的模式，最有代表性的是南北

painting, there is a yellow loong; on its right side, there is a white deer; the left bottom presents a double trunk tree under which a man is holding a plate to get the nectar. Besides, a magic crop seedling is in the middle of the tree.

Auspice culture further developed in the Wei, Jin, the Southern and Northern dynasties (220-589) when a number of fixed features of auspicious animals were formed. The most representative relevant work is *Ruiying Tu* (*Pictures of Auspicious Animals and Birds*) written in the Southern and Northern dynasties (386-589). Over 100 images and their

- 青瓷狮形器（西晋）
  Lion-shaped Celadon Porcelain Vessel (Western Jin Dynasty, 265-317)

- 青瓷鸡窝（晋）
  Celadon Porcelain Henhouse (Jin Dynasty, 265-420)

• 手工缝制的虎头鞋
Hand-made Tiger-head Shoes

朝时期的《瑞应图》一书，对前代流传下来的一百多种具有祥瑞寓意的物象进行汇集并绘成图录。到了隋、唐、宋时期，祥瑞文化异常兴盛。在陶瓷、染织、金银器、漆器、家具、石雕等的装饰上，都出现了祥瑞动物的形象。除了传说中的龙、凤等"神兽"，鹿、喜鹊、鸡等常见动物也被加入了瑞兽、祥禽的行列。这些动物的形象与之前相比更加富丽堂皇、气韵生动。唐人刘赓著有《稽瑞》一书，书中收录了185种民间的吉祥物。

明清时期，祥瑞文化的发展达到顶峰，各种有关瑞兽、祥禽的吉祥

auspicious meanings handed down from previous periods were recorded in the book. In the Sui, Tang and Song dynasties (581-1279), auspice culture gained even greater popularity. Their images were used as decoration for various objects like pottery and porcelain wares, clothing, golden and silver wares, lacquer wares, furniture, stone carvings, etc. In addition to legendary creatures like loong and phoenix, ordinary animals such as deer, magpie and rooster were also included in the range of auspicious creatures, the images of which became even more splendid and lively. Besides, Liu Geng of the Tang Dynasty (618-907), authored a book named *Ji Rui* (*Interesting AuspiciousAnimals and Birds*) in which 185 popular auspicious creatures and signs in folk culture were described.

The development of auspice culture peaked in the Ming and Qing dynasties (1368-1911) when various verbal phrases and images relating to them prevailed. They were so popular that nearly each painting shall include a meaning, and each meaning shall refer to propitiousness. Auspicious decoration existed in nearly every aspect of life. They were everywhere on constructions, daily wares, utensils and clothing.

- 羚羊首玛瑙杯（唐）
Agate Cup with Design of Antelope Head (Tang Dynasty, 618-907)

- 碧玉鱼龙形花插（清）

鱼龙变化又称"鱼跃龙门"。传说中的"龙门"位于黄河的龙门山上，鲤鱼只要跳过龙门就会化身为龙。"鱼跃龙门"常用来祝愿读书人在科举考试中一举夺魁、金榜题名。

Jasper Fish-loong-shaped Flower Receptacle (Qing Dynasty, 1616-1911)
Fish-loong transformation, also known as "Fish leaping over the Loong Gate", was a legend that when the carp leaped over the Loong Gate which was located on the Loong Gate Mountain of Yellow River, it could transform into a loong. This idiom is used as wishes to intellectuals for their success in getting the first place in the final civil servant exam.

语和吉祥图案在社会上非常流行，几乎到了"图必有意，意必吉祥"的程度。从建筑到日用品、服装等，几乎生活的每个角落都有吉祥图案装饰的存在。龙、凤形象变得异常繁复而富贵，成为皇家的专用图案，以彰显皇家的气派；狮、鹤等图案被用来区分官级的大小，保佑官运的亨通；民间用虎头鞋、兔儿帽作为儿童的鞋帽，寄托了父母对孩子健康、活泼成长的愿望。

Loong and phoenix gradually turned into sophisticated forms and symbolized the supreme power of the royal family. Images like lions and cranes were used to distinguish ranks of government officials and to bring good luck to their way to higher ranks. Tiger-head shoes and rabbit-shaped hats were popular among children, showing their parents' wishes to offer them a happy and healthy childhood.

瑞兽
Auspicious Animals

中国传统文化中有吉祥寓意的瑞兽种类很多。有的是神话中虚构的动物，比如龙和麒麟，是传说中太平盛世的象征；也有的在现实中真实存在，比如象、牛、羊等，给人们的生活带来了切实的帮助。

There are a variety of auspicious animals that have propitious connotations in traditional Chinese culture. Some of them are fictional animals in mythology, such as the loong and the kylin that symbolize peace and prosperity; others exist in reality, such as elephant, ox and sheep that can bring practical help to people's lives.

> 华夏图腾——龙

龙是中国古代传说中一种神奇的动物。根据古籍记载，龙具有鹿的角、马的头、牛的耳朵、兔的眼，蛇的身体、鱼的鳞、鹰的爪子。中国人相信，龙具有神奇的力量，不仅可以腾云驾雾、兴云布

> China's Totem: Loong

Loong is a magical creature in ancient Chinese legends. According to ancient records, it has the antlers of the deer, the head of the horse, the ears of the ox, the eyes of the rabbit, the body of the snake, the scales of the fish and the claws of the eagle. Ancient Chinese believed that loong is endowed with magical power. It is not only able to fly in the sky, to summon clouds and rain, but also to dispel disasters. Since ancient times, Chinese people have made loong as their totem and claimed themselves to be the descendants of the loong.

- 红山文化"C"形玉龙（新石器时代）
C-shaped Jade Loong from the Hongshan Culture (The Neolithic Age, approx. 8000 years ago)

雨，而且能消除灾难。自古以来，中国人就以龙为图腾，一向自称"龙的子孙"。

早在原始社会的新石器时代，就出现了带有龙的特征的动物形象和纹饰，被称为"原龙纹"。辽宁阜新查海原始村落遗址出土的龙形堆塑距今约8000年，由大小均等的红褐色石块堆塑而成，全长近20米，昂首又张口，弯腰又弓背，尾部若隐若现，是中国迄今发现的最早的龙的造型。原龙纹的形象没有双角，与今天人们印象中的龙的形象有很大的差距。

到了商代，作为祭祀礼器的青铜器上出现了带角的龙纹，商代人

As early as in primitive societies during the Neolithic Age (approx. 8000 years ago), animal images and patterns that had characteristics of the loong existed, known as the original loong pattern. A loong-shaped rock-fill built about 8,000 years ago was unearthed from ruins of the primitive villages in Chahai of Fuxin City, Liaoning Province. It is made of reddish brown stones of equal size and is nearly 20 meters long with an open mouth, a curved body, an arched back and an indistinct tail. It is the earliest Chinese loong pattern discovered so far, which is different from the loong patterns in people's impression nowadays for it has no antlers.

In the Shang Dynasty (1600 B.C.-1046 B.C.), antlers were added to the images of the loong that were incised on bronze wares used in the rite of sacrifice. Besides, features of other animals, like elephant, tiger, pig and crocodile, were added to the loong image so that it could be different from any other animal in the world. The loong in the Shang Dynasty

- 龙纹扁足青铜鼎（商）
Flatfeet Bronze Tripod with Loong Pattern (Shang Dynasty, 1600 B.C.-1046 B.C.)

龙形玉饰（战国）
Loong-shaped Jade Ornament (Warring States Period, 475 B.C.-221 B.C.)

还将象、虎、猪、鳄等动物的不同特征加到龙的身上，从而使龙成为不同于世间任何一种动物的"神兽"。商代的龙具有一种狞厉的美，显示出龙具有"神"的权威。

西周建立后，各种礼器上龙的形象趋于弱化，故此时龙的体态少了张扬、狞厉的慑人气势，变得比较平和，更趋于艺术化和图案化。春秋战国时期，随着社会的动荡，以及思想、艺术的自由，龙的形象摆脱了拘谨、划一的格局，风格更加新巧、精细而富于变化。

汉代的皇帝将传说中的龙作为彰显皇权

透雕双龙纹玉璧（西汉）
Hollow Carved Jade Plate with Double Loongs Pattern (Western Han Dynasty, 206 B.C.-25 A.D.)

has a ferocious beauty, demonstrating that its supreme power.

After the establishment of the Western Zhou Dynasty (1046 B.C.-771 B.C.), the loong became gentle, changing from its pretentious and ferocious look to a more peaceful appearance, showing the trend towards more artistic and patterning style. With social unrest and freedom of thoughts and art during the Spring and Autumn Period (770 B.C.-476 B.C.) and the Warring States Period (475 B.C.-221 B.C.), the loong gradually transformed from a reserved and unified form to a more novel, refined and diverse image.

Emperors of the Han Dynasty (206 B.C.-220 A.D.) used the legendary dragon as a tool to show imperial power. Thus, the image of the loong

• 云龙纹铜镜（唐）
Bronze Mirror with Cloud and Loong Pattern (Tang Dynasty, 618-907)

的工具，龙的形象具有凌厉的动势和豪迈的气魄，在造型上简化了细节，而更注重神采。南北朝时期，佛教盛行，龙的形象风格由汉代那种粗犷、奔放转为宁静、洒脱、俊俏，龙的体形被拉长，表现出一种超凡脱俗的意境。

隋唐到两宋时期，经济快速发展，中国社会达到了封建社会繁荣的高峰，而这一时期的龙也充满了精神气魄和生活气息。无论是绘画、陶瓷，还是建筑装饰上的龙纹图案，其神情和瞬间动作变化的塑

was more aggressive, heroic and brave. Details were simplified, but the gist was highlighted. As Buddhism prevailed during the Southern and Northern dynasties (386-589), the image of the rough and unrestrained loong in the Han Dynasty was replaced with a quiet, smart and handsome one. Besides, the body of the loong was elongated to demonstrate a spiritual disposition.

During the Sui, Tang and Song dynasties (581-1279), China's feudal society reached its zenith of prosperity due to the rapid development of society and economy. In this period, the image of the loong was full of the spirit of boldness and life. Loong patterns used on paintings, porcelain wares and buildings were usually extremely vivid with lifelike expressions and poses. As a kind of imaginary animals, its image was nearly perfect.

In the Yuan, Ming and Qing dynasties (1206-1911), except for a few minor changes, the loong remained similar to its previous image. Before the Yuan Dynasty (1206-1368), the four claws of the loong only had three fingers on each. From the Yuan Dynasty, however, three-finger and four-finger loong-like images were known as the python. Only the five-finger one

- 青花云龙纹罐（元）

Blue-and-white (*Qinghua*) Jar with Cloud and Loong Pattern (Yuan Dynasty, 1206-1368)

- 五彩团龙纹罐（明）

Polychrome Jar with Loong in Circle Pattern (Ming Dynasty, 1368-1644)

造都极为生动，龙作为一种想象中的动物，其形象已臻完善。

元、明、清三代，龙的造型基本上没有重大的改变。元代以前的龙纹，龙的四足大多是三爪形的。

was regarded as the loong and could only be used by the emperors and the royal family.

One of the basic features of the loong is its ability to control the rain and fly on clouds. The earliest image of the loong

端午节赛龙舟

端午节是中国古老的传统节日之一，时间在每年的农历五月初五。在这一天，人们用包粽子、饮雄黄酒、赛龙舟来庆祝节日，尤以赛龙舟最为热闹。传说赛龙舟起源于古代吴越地区举行的图腾祭祀活动，百姓为了求得龙的护佑，把船雕刻成龙形，在水面上进行竞赛活动。龙舟长十四五米，形状狭长，宽度为仅能容纳两个人并排坐下。比赛时一般20人组成一组，分两排坐在舟中，每人手拿一

> 仁德高贵——麒麟

麒麟是中国古代传说中的"神兽",初时雄者为"麒",雌者为"麟",后来不分雄雌,统称"麒麟"。麒麟也是众多动物的集合体,麋身、牛尾、马蹄、鱼鳞皮,头上有肉角,口能吐火,声音很大,而且能使人逢凶化吉。人们对

• 孔子像
Portrait of Confucius

> Noble Spirit: Kylin

Kylin also named *Qilin* is a magical creature in ancient Chinese mythology. Originally, the male one was named *Qi*, while the female one was named *Lin*. Nevertheless, people stopped distinguishing their genders, and simply referred to them as kylin later. Kylin is also an embodiment of several animals, including the body of the moose, the tail of the ox, the hooves of the horse and the scales of the fish. It has fleshy antlers on its head. Its mouth could spit out fire and roar like thunder. It could foretell disasters to save people from them. The earliest worship of kylin began in the Spring and Autumn Period (770 B.C.-476 B.C.). In *The Book of Songs*, which first published in the Spring and Autumn Period, is a collection of poems written in the Pre-Qin Period. In this book, there is a poem, named *Toes of the Kylin* in

只船桨，有节奏地用力划行；船头一人手拿彩旗负责指挥，船尾还有一名鼓手，以鼓声激励士气。比赛开始后，在锣鼓和鞭炮的助威下，各条龙舟离弦之箭一般向前划行，劈波斩浪，两岸观众则齐声呐喊，气氛十分热烈。

Loong Boat Racing in Loong Boat Festival

According to the lunar calendar, every year's fifth day of the fifth month is the Loong Boat Festival, one of the most ancient Chinese festivals. Its celebration traditions usually include eating steamed glutinous rice wrapped in bamboo leaves, drinking realgar wine and the loong boat racing, among which the boat racing is the most exciting one. The loong boat racing originated from the rite of sacrifice in the ancient Wu-Yue area (now around Zhejiang Province and Jiangsu Province). Loong-shaped boats would race on the river to show worship of the loong and to pray for its blessing. The loong boat is usually fourteen to fifteen meters long and is too narrow to hold more than two persons sitting side by side. In each boat, there are about 20 people sitting in two rows and each of them would hold a paddle to row rhythmically. Besides, each team has a commander holding a colorful flag in the front and a drummer to keep their morale up at the back of the boat. When the race starts, each loong boat would move forward like arrows and cleave through the water with great fever accompanied by the loud sound of drums and firecrackers, as well as the cheering from the audience on the banks, creating an exciting atmosphere.

- 端午节的龙舟赛
  Boat Racing on Loong Boat Festival

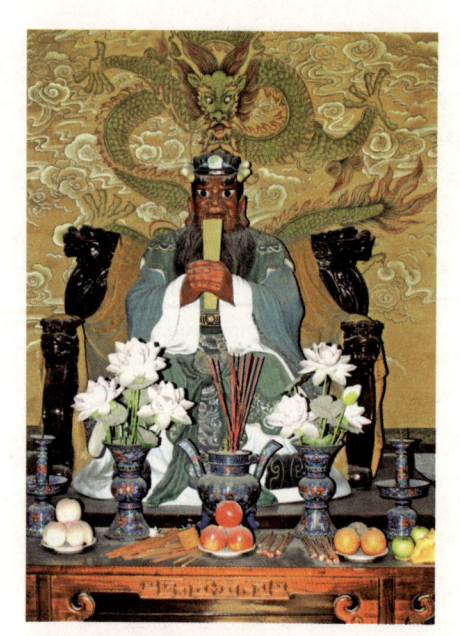

• 龙王庙中供奉的龙王像
Statue of the Loong King in a Loong King Temple

从元代开始，三爪、四爪龙被称为"蟒"，只有五爪龙才被称为"龙"，仅限皇帝及皇室使用。

能够兴云布雨、腾云驾雾是龙最基本的特征之一。在龙的形象形成之初，人们就将龙当作云、雷电、虹霓等空中种种天象的化身，龙既能在水中游，在地上跑，也能在天上飞。龙还司雨水。中国是传统的农业大国，良好的天气和合理的降水对农业生产的影响很大。在古代中国，

was the embodiment of the weather, such as cloud, lightning, thunder and rainbow, so it was described as a magical creature that can swim in the water, run on the ground, and fly in the sky. It was also said to be the Loong King who was in charge of the rain and water. As agriculture was the dominant industry in ancient China, a good harvest was essential to socio-economic prosperity, but it largely depended on nice weather conditions. Therefore, temples of the Loong King have been built everywhere in ancient China. When drought happened, people would pray for rain from the Loong King to save the world.

The loong's capability of flying freely came from ancient Chinese's ideal of exceeding the limitations of humans and getting rid of earthly ordeal. As the loong can fly, it was often described as the mount of immortals in the Heaven. Unearthed from tombs of the Chu State in Changsha, Hunan Province during the Warring States Period, there was a silk painting *Riding the Loong*. Besides, similar paintings with an immortal riding on the loong were also discovered on portrait bricks of the Han Dynasty.

For ancient Chinese, the loong is also a symbol of propitiousness. It was

• 青花鱼龙变化纹洗涤器（清）
Blue-and-white (*Qinghua*) Porcelain Brush Washer with Fish-loong Transformation Pattern (Qing Dynasty, 1616-1911)

• "人物驭龙"帛画（战国）
Silk Painting *Riding the Loong* (Warring States Period, 475 B.C.-221 B.C.)

大江南北都建有龙王庙，每逢大旱之时，人们就会前往龙王庙祈求龙王降下甘霖，解救苍生。

能够在天空中自由飞腾的龙寄托了古人超越自身局限、摆脱现世苦累的愿望。由于龙可以飞翔，自然就成了传说中天上"神仙"的坐骑。湖南长沙的战国楚墓中就出土了"人物驭龙"帛画，汉代的画像砖上也有"仙人乘龙图"。

对古代中国人来说，龙还是祥瑞的象征，人们把龙当作能够带

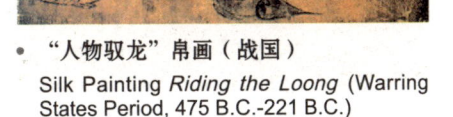

considered as an auspicious animal that can bring good luck and happiness.

After the Qin Dynasty (221 B.C.-206 B.C.) and the Han Dynasty, the loong became a symbol of the imperial power. The emperors considered themselves the proud son of heaven. As an auspicious creature with magical powers in legend, the loong was known for its ability to bring benefits to the people. Emperors thought their monarchical power was divine and they shouldered the mission to save the people from disasters and give

• 北京故宫太极殿影壁上的云龙图案
Cloud and Loong Decoration on Taiji Hall of the Forbidden City, Beijing

来吉祥、幸福的瑞兽。

秦汉以后，龙开始成为帝王皇权的象征。皇帝自认为是天之骄子。传说中，龙有兆瑞的"神性"，是能够给天下人带来好处的"神物"。帝王们也都认为自己的君权是"神"授的，肩负着救民于水火、解民于倒悬的使命。于是，龙的神性与帝王的权力在此结合，皇帝被称为龙的后代——"真龙天子"，所用的

happiness to them. Thus, the divinity of the loong and the power of the emperors overlapped and were combined together. Emperors were known as descendants of the loong—real loong from the Heaven, and everything related to emperors contained the word "loong". For example, the Emperor's clothes were called loong robes or loong imperial robes; the Emperor's seat was referred to as the seat of the loong; the Emperor's

龙生九子

中国民间流传着"龙生九子，子子不同"的俗语，这个说法大约起源于明代，人们汇集了古代各种文献中的怪异"神兽"，将它们归为龙子，作为建筑、器物或重要场所的装饰纹样，让它们"各司一职"，为人们消除灾难。一般经常提到的龙子有赑屃、螭吻、狴犴、蒲牢、饕餮、睚眦、狻猊、椒图、貔貅等。

Nine Sons of the Loong

As a Chinese idiom goes, the loong has nine sons and they all have different appearances and personalities. This saying may have originated in the Ming Dynasty (1368-1644). This folklore brings together strange mythical creatures in ancient literature and regards them as sons of the loong. Each of them has different functions and they are also used as ornamentation for constructions, artifacts and important venues so as to avoid misfortune and disasters. *Bixi, Chiwen, Bi'an, Pulao, Taotie, Yazi, Suanni, Jiaotu* and *Pixiu* were among the most frequently seen creatures.

• 古代建筑大门上的"椒图"辅首

椒图的形象像螺蚌，性好闭口，不喜欢别人或者外物入侵它的巢穴，所以经常作为大门的装饰，据说可以保佑宅院安宁。

Jiaotu Knocker on an Ancient Door

It says that *Jiaotu* looks like the mussel. It was quiet and protective towards its home. Thus, it was often used as a decoration for doors to keep peace in the house.

• 彩绘陶辟邪（汉）

辟邪的形象为龙头、马身，大嘴，无肛门，头上有角，以金银为食，又名"天禄""貔貅"，传说可招财进宝。

Coloured Pottery *Bixie* (Han Dynasty, 206 B.C.-220 A.D.)

Bixie has the head of the loong, the body of the horse and a big mouth, two antlers, but it doesn't have an anal. It is also known as *Tianlu* or *Pixiu*. As it is said to have gold and silver as food, it symbolizes bringing in money and treasures.

● 古代建筑正脊上的螭吻

螭吻的形象为长有鱼尾的龙，生性喜欢站在高处眺望，据说可以降雨、灭火等，所以人们常把它雕刻在房屋的屋脊处。

Chiwen on the Main Beam of an Antique Building

Chiwen is described to be a loong with the tail of fish. It enjoys gazing down from a high place, making the rain and keeping the house from fire. Thus, it is often carved on the roof of the house.

● 饕餮纹瓦当（战国）

饕餮是一种生性贪吃的怪兽。饕餮纹也称"兽面纹"，盛行于商代及西周早期。

Eaves Tile with *Taotie* Pattern (Warring States Period, 475 B.C.-221 B.C.)

Taotie is seen as a gluttonous monster. *Taotie* pattern, also known as beast face pattern, was popular in the Shang Dynasty (1600 B.C.-1046 B.C.) and early Western Zhou Dynasty.

• 身着龙袍的清康熙帝像
Portrait of Emperor Kangxi in His Loong Robe

东西一律被冠以"龙"字。皇帝的衣服叫"龙袍""龙衮",皇帝的座位叫"龙座",皇帝的床叫"龙床";皇帝即位后叫"龙飞",登基前叫"龙潜";皇帝高兴是"龙颜大悦",有病则是"龙体欠安"。

到了元、明、清三代,龙的地位被抬到无以复加的高度。

• 饰有龙纹的御用墨(清)
Imperial Ink Stick with the Loong Pattern (Qing Dynasty, 1616-1911)

bed was named the bed of the loong; the Emperor's ascending throne was fly of the loong, and the period before ascending the throne was dive of the loong; when the Emperor was happy, it was a sign of happy loong face; when the Emperor was sick, this was phrased as the loong is unwell.

In the Yuan Dynasty, the Ming Dynasty (1368-1644) and the Qing Dynasty (1616-1911), the status of the loong was pushed to an extreme height.

- 北京故宫保和殿里的龙椅
Loong Seat in Hall Preserving Harmony in the Forbidden City, Beijing

二月二龙抬头

在中国，每年农历二月初二被称为"春龙节"，传说是天上主管云雨的龙王抬头苏醒的日子。民间有"二月二，龙抬头"的谚语，表示春季来临，万物复苏，预示一年的农事活动即将开始。二月二这一天的民间饮食多以"龙"为名，如吃水饺叫"吃龙耳"，吃米饭叫"吃龙子"，吃馄饨叫"吃龙眼"，吃面条叫"扶龙须"。北方人做蒸饼，也要在面上做出龙鳞状来，称"龙鳞饼"。中国人还相信，在这一天理发，会使人鸿运当头、福星高照，因此有民谚说："二月二剃龙头，一年都有精神头。"这些习俗寄托了人们祈求龙赐福，保佑风调雨顺、五谷丰登的美好愿望。

Waking of the Loong on the Second Day of the Second Month

In China, the second day of the second month in the lunar calendar is known as the Spring Loong Festival. According to folk legends, it is on that day that the Loong King in charge of cloud and rain wakes up and looks up to the sky. The proverb Rise of the Loong means that spring is coming and everything will be resurrected, which shows the start of farming activities. Names of food and snacks that people have on that day begin with the word loong. For example, boiled dumplings are called loong ears; rice is loong sons; wontons are loong eyes, and noodles are loong beards. In Northern China, people would make loong scales on steamed cakes. Besides, people believe that having a haircut on that day will bring good luck and blessings, as it was said "Shaving on the second day of the second month, good luck is with you for a whole year". These customs show people's cravings for blessings from the loong so that they can have nice weather conditions and good harvests.

• 青花麒麟芭蕉纹盘（清）
Blue-and-white (*Qinghua*) Porcelain Plate with Kylin and Banana Leaves Pattern (Qing Dynasty, 1616-1911)

麒麟的崇拜始于春秋时期。在成书于春秋时期的先秦诗歌总集《诗经》的《周南》一章中，有一首诗叫《麟之趾》，诗中将贵族公子比作"神兽"麒麟，将公子的美德比作麒麟的趾爪、额头和双角。可见在那时，人们已经把麒麟看作美德和高贵的象征。

　　传说中，麒麟的寿命很长，性情温和，"不践生草，不履生虫"，被称为"仁兽"，只有天下太平的丰收之年，它才会出现，所以它的出现常带有祥瑞、福禄的含义。古人将麒麟与圣人联系在一起。相传在春秋末期的鲁国，儒家

Chapter of Zhounan (which is an ancient Chinese country). According to the poem, the nobility childe was praised as the magical creature kylin and his virtues were seen as its claws, forehead, and antlers. Apparently, kylin was considered as the symbol of virtue and nobleness at that time.

　　According to legends, kylin tends to live a very long life and it has a mild temperament. Kylin is said to be a benevolent animal that is too kind to trample on green grass and living insects. It would not appear in the human world unless the world enjoyed a good harvest with peace. Thus, kylin was often connected with the meaning of good luck and fortune. Besides, it was often related to sages. It is said that on the night before Confucius was born during the Spring and Autumn Period (770 B.C.-476 B.C.), a kylin appeared in the courtyard of his parents' home in the State of Lu. It spits out a jade scroll from its mouth. On the scroll, it wrote: "A man of extraordinary good moral character and talent, an exemplar of human excellence. When the Eastern Zhou Dynasty (770 B.C.-256 B.C.) falls, he can possibly be an uncrowned king." It means that a sage who would not be an emperor, but having

学派创始人孔子出生前的那天夜里，一头麒麟来到孔家，嘴里吐出一方玉书，上面写着："水精之子孙，衰周而素王。"意思是有个圣人将要降世，他虽未居帝王之位，却有帝王之德。不久，孔子就降生了。

如果说龙是帝王的象征，那么麒麟则多被人们与将相、功臣联系在一起。西汉时期，汉武帝曾在皇宫未央宫内建"麒麟阁"，并在阁

all the virtues of the emperor was to be born. Not long after its appearance, Confucius was born.

While the loong was the symbol of emperors, the kylin was often related to outstanding generals and officials. In the Western Han Dynasty (206 B.C.-25 A.D), Emperor Wu (156 B.C.-87 B.C.) built a Kylin Tower in his Weiyang Forbidden City, where portraits of influential generals and court officials were hung as reward and showcase of how important they were to the imperial court. Kylin patterns also appeared on officials' robes. For example, in the Qing Dynasty (1616-1911), robes tailored for top-grade court officials were embroidered with kylin patterns. This was an indication that their status ranked second only to the emperor who was symbolized by the loong.

Not only royal families attached importance to the kylin, ordinary people also liked it. *Qi* or *Lin* was among the most popular names that parents gave to newborn babies to wish them to be bright and brave like the kylin. Children would wear kylin hats and kylin locks, so that they could have a longevity and healthy life. When a girl got married, she would receive a kylin-pattern talisman bag containing jewelries or money from

• 《麒麟送子》年画
New Year Picture with Kylin Delivers a Boy Pattern

- 银制"麒麟送子"长命锁（清）

  人们根据孔子与麒麟的传说创作了"麒麟送子"图案，流传十分广泛。民间普遍相信，求拜麒麟能为人们带来子嗣。

  Silver Longevity Lock with Kylin Sending the Son Pattern (Qing Dynasty, 1616-1911)

  Kylin Sending the Son pattern was created based on the legend of Confucius and the kylin. It was extremely popular in folk culture and most people believed that kylin's blessing brings offspring.

内绘制功臣像，作为对功臣的嘉奖，以表示朝廷对他们的重视。麒麟图案也常出现在官服上，清代一品官的官服上就有麒麟图案，地位仅次于龙。

皇家重视、喜爱麒麟，民间亦然。百姓给孩子取名时常采用"麒"或者"麟"字，希望给孩子带来福气，使孩子聪慧、勇敢。孩子小的时候会戴麒麟帽，挂麒麟锁，据说可以保佑孩子健康成长、长命百岁。女孩出嫁时，母亲往往送给她们绣有麒麟的锦袋，里面装有珠宝首饰或金钱，以祝福女儿婚后生活富裕，早生贵子。关于麒麟的成语也多是褒义的，如用"麟肝凤髓"比喻美味佳肴，用"麟子凤雏"比喻英俊少年，等等。

her mother as a wedding gift to wish her a well-off marriage and lovely kids as soon as possible. Most idioms about kylin carry positive connotations. For instance, liver of the kylin and marrow of the phoenix refers to delicious food; descendant of the kylin and offspring of the phoenix means handsome young men.

> 镇宅驱邪——虎

虎在中国传统的祥瑞动物中占有重要的地位，仅次于龙。《周易·乾卦》"文言"中就有"云从龙，风从虎"的记载，龙飞于天，虎行于地，虎与龙结合在一起，成为吉祥和权威的象征。以虎为图腾

• 双虎纹瓦当（战国）
Eaves Tile with Double Tigers Pattern (Warring States Period, 475 B.C.-221 B.C.)

> Home-guarding Exorcist: Tiger

Tiger occupies an important place in traditional Chinese auspicious animals. Its status is only second to the loong. It was written in *Interpretation of Qian* in the book named *Zhouyi* (also known as the *Book of Change* or *Yi Jing*) that cloud is with the loong, while the wind is with the tiger. The loong that could fly in the sky and the tiger that could run on the ground became a symbol of luck and authority. Worship of the tiger totem was popular in primitive societies. Many clans and tribes worshiped the tiger as their ancestor or patron.

In the view of the ancient Chinese, tiger, the feline creature is mighty and brutal. It was feared and hated by people, but also respected and admired. In ancient times, brave generals were praised as brave as the tiger; people who are full of vigor and vitality are known

• 陕西凤翔泥塑挂虎
Tiger Made by Technique of Fengxiang Clay Figurine of Shaanxi Province

的崇拜在原始社会十分盛行，许多氏族和部落把虎视为自己的祖先或保护神而顶礼膜拜。

在古人心中，老虎这种猫科动物威猛而又凶残，让人既畏惧、憎恨，又忍不住崇敬、爱慕。古代作战勇猛的武将被称为"虎将"；形容一个人很有活力的样子称"生龙活虎""虎虎生风"；形容小男孩可爱，说他长得"虎头虎脑"。唐宋时期，皇帝身边的近卫军被称

as energetic as the tiger and as talented as the tiger; smart kid are described as having a tiger head and a tiger brain. During the Tang Dynasty (618-907) and the Song Dynasty (960-1279), squires close to the emperor were renowned as tiger warriors. Ying Shao of the Eastern Han Dynasty (25-220) wrote in his book *Fengsu Tongyi* (*Custom Links*) that if you paint a tiger on the door, even ghosts dare not get into the room. Tiger was used as mascot to dispel disasters. Thus, tiger

• 虎镇五毒纹肚兜（清）

肚兜是一种保护胸、腹部的贴身内衣。"五毒"象征各种毒虫，以虎镇之，意味着驱逐瘟病，祈求安康。这件肚兜将五毒的形象拟人化，头部及上身表现为身着彩衣的女子，下半部仍是毒虫形象，显得妙趣横生。

Dudou (a Piece of Underwear Covering the Abdomen and the Chest) with Tiger and Five Poisonous Creatures Pattern (Qing Dynasty, 1616-1911)

Dudou is a type of underwear that warms the chest and belly. Five poisonous creatures refer to scorpion, viper, centipede, house lizard and toad. Tiger cracking down on them implies banishing sickness and praying for good health. The five poisonous creatures were personified as they have female head with their upper body dressed up in colorful clothes, but their lower body revealed their identities as poisonous creatures, making the picture full of humor and wit.

为"虎贲军"。东汉人应劭在《风俗通义》中写道："画虎于门，鬼不敢入。"古代民间将老虎当作镇宅、避灾的吉祥物。在青铜器、建筑装饰上经常能看到老虎的形象。人们尤其喜欢把老虎当作孩子们的守护神，让孩子穿虎头鞋、戴虎头帽、睡虎头枕，希望孩子在老虎的庇护下健康长大。

ornaments can often be seen on bronze wares and constructions. Besides, tiger was regarded as the guardian of children. Thus, parents would give their children tiger-head shoes, tiger-head hats, and tiger-head pillows to help their children grow up healthily under the protection of the tiger.

> 百兽之王——狮

对古代中国人来说，狮子是外来的动物。狮子原产于亚洲西部和非洲，于汉代时传入中国。据史料记载，东汉章和元年（87年），月氏国国王派商队沿丝绸之路把狮子作为礼物献给汉章帝。狮子传入中国后，以其威严的外表和凶猛的习性受到中国人的尊崇，甚至动摇了虎在人们心目中的地位。

东汉时期的石雕狮子一般呈行走状，昂头挺胸，张嘴怒吼，目光逼人，刻工简练而粗犷，具有古拙的风味。唐代以前的狮子雕塑通常与老虎十分相近，难以分辨。同时代常见的辟邪、天禄、麒麟等形象

- 走狮石雕（唐）
  Stone Sculpture of a Walking Lion (Tang Dynasty, 618-907)

> King of All Animals: Lion

For ancient Chinese, the lion was an exotic animal. It originated from the West Asia and Africa and was brought to China in the Han Dynasty (206 B.C.-220 A.D.). According to historical records, a caravan sent by the King of

都不同程度地呈现出狮形。到了唐代，狮子的造型更有气魄，雕琢更为精美。唐代出现了大量蹲坐式的石狮，其前肢斜伸，胸部挺起，狮头高昂，具有一种慑人的气势。宋代，人们开始在狮子的颈部配上铃铛、绶带，狮子的形象变得

Yuezhi travelled through the Silk Road and brought a lion as a gift to Emperor Zhang who just inherited the throne (87) during the Eastern Han Dynasty (25-220). When ancient Chinese first saw the lion, they were impressed by its majestic appearance and fierce characteristic. People liked it so much that the status of the tiger wavered.

Stone lions in the Eastern Han Dynasty were generally in the poise of walking with its head tilting slightly upwards and its body facing forwards, its mouth opening and eyes threatening. They were carved with simple and rough techniques and were in primitive and crude styles. Lion sculptures made before the Tang Dynasty (618-907) had similar appearance with the tiger. Thus, it was hard to tell whether it was a lion or a tiger. The lion to different degrees influenced images of *Bixie*, *Tianlu* and kylin from the same era. In the Tang Dynasty, the lion was shaped in higher spirits with more exquisite carving techniques. Many squatting stone lions appeared in the Tang Dynasty. With a

- 北京故宫乾清门前的铜狮
Copper Lion beside the Qianqing Gate of the Forbidden City, Beijing

- **青花釉里红狮球纹瓷瓶（清）**

"狮子滚绣球"是民间十分流行的装饰纹样。传说雌、雄二狮相戏时，它们的毛纠缠在一起，滚成毛球，小狮子便从球中产出，这就是"绣球"的来历。

Red Underglazed Blue-and-white (*Qinghua*) Porcelain Vase with the Lion Playing with the Silk Ball Pattern (Qing Dynasty, 1616-1911)

The Lion Playing with the Silk Ball is a popular folk decorative pattern. According to the legend, when a male lion plays with the female lion, their hair would entangle together and then roll into a ball from which a lion cub would be born. That was the origin of the silk ball.

乖巧、温顺起来。明、清两代，狮子的造型基本定型，成为现在常见的形象：姿势为蹲坐式，前腿支撑有力，后腿盘曲稳固，头部的鬣毛被整齐地圈成漩涡状。这种造型的狮子在很多宫殿、寺庙、官衙的大门前都能被看到。在民间织绣、刺绣、印染、年画、剪纸、陶瓷中也有很多狮子造型，这些狮子大多被突出了玩赏性，变得像宠物般可爱，失去了威风凛凛的气质。

fearful bearing, their forelimbs stretched on one side, chest straightened, and head tilted upward. In the Song Dynasty (960-1279), people started to create well-behaved images of the lion with bells and ribbons tied on its neck. The lion obtained its stereotype in the Ming and Qing dynasties (1368-1911). A typical lion sculpture would have a squatting posture and swirled mane, with stretched front legs and twisted back legs. We can see this type of stone lions beside the gates of palaces, temples, and antique government offices. Besides, lion ornaments also appear on wove cloth, embroidery, printed and dyed cloth, Spring Festival pictures, paper-cuts, and ceramic wares. Most of these lions show their playfulness and they look more like lovely pets than awe-inspiring beasts.

舞狮子

　　舞狮自古就是人们喜闻乐见的一种表演形式。据《汉书》记载,汉代时,民间就已经开始流行舞狮子,两个人扮成一头狮子,一个人拿着绣球与狮子戏耍。每逢节日,人们就会表演狮子滚绣球。两人一组扮成狮子,一人举狮头,一人托狮身;第三个人手拿绣球来逗狮子。舞狮常用彩线作为装饰,线条流畅,舞狮的人身手矫健,不时让狮子做一些可爱或者惊险的动作,使得狮子看起来喜气洋洋,惹人喜爱。人们相信看到狮子能带来好运,所以一旦有舞狮活动,观看者就会特别多。

Lion Dance

Lion dance is a popular form of performance since ancient times. According to *Han Shu* (*History of the Han Dynasty*), the lion dance prevailed in the Han Dynasty. It refers to two men dressing up as a lion, while another man holding a silk ball to play with the lion. This performance of Lion Playing with the Silk Ball almost never misses any festival. The lion is usually made up of two men, with one man holding the head, and the other holding the body. A silk ball is held by another man to tease the lion. The fake lion was often decorated with color threads and had smooth structure. Agile lion dancers liked to show lovely or thrilling movements to make the lion full of joy and adorable. As it was said that seeing the lion could bring good luck, the lion dance usually appealed to many viewers.

● 民间舞狮表演（图片提供：全景正片）
Folk Lion Dance Performance

> 勇猛矫捷——豹

豹的体形与虎相似，但较小，属于大中型食肉动物。古代时，豹在中国各地都有广泛的分布，分东北豹、华北豹和华南豹三个种类。目前只有华南豹在湖南、江西、福建、广东、贵州、四川等地的一些偏远山区还有种群分布，但数量已急剧减少。

中国的豹浑身毛色多为鲜亮的棕黄色，遍布黑色斑点和环纹，近似古代的圆形方孔钱，所以中国人称之为"金钱豹"。豹纹绚丽多彩，故豹深受古人喜爱，很多饰物上都有豹纹的图案。如在赤黄色的布上绘有豹纹的装饰物称为"豹尾"，是权威和荣誉的象征，通常饰于仪仗上。悬豹尾的车叫作"豹尾车"，是皇帝车队的最后一辆。

> Agile Warrior: Leopard

Leopard is a type of large and medium-sized predator, but compared with the tiger it is smaller. In ancient times, the leopard widely spread throughout China. Three subspecies used to exist, including the Northeast China Leopard (P.p.orientalis), the North China Leopard (P.p.fontanieri) and the South China Leopard (P.pardus fusea). Currently, only the South China Leopard (P.pardus fusea) survives in remote mountainous areas in Hunan, Jiangxi, Fujian, Guangdong, Guizhou and Sichuan provinces, and their number suffered from sharp decline in recent years.

Most Chinese leopards have bright yellowish brown color with dark speckles and circular stripes all over their body, which resemble the ancient Chinese coins that had a round rim and a square hole in the center. Hence, the leopard is

• 错金银铜豹（战国）
Bronze Leopard with Inlaid Gold and Silver (Warring States Period, 475 B.C.- 221 B.C.)

also known as the golden money leopard. Ancient Chinese loved this bright and colorful leopard print and used it on a variety of objects. For example, the leopard tail that had the leopard print on a ginger color cloth represented authority and honor. The cart with the leopard tail, namely the leopard tail cart, was usually the last cart in such procession.

Leopard is not only a fierce warrior, but also a strategist who is good at hiding. Thus, it represents not only braveness, but also military strategy. *Liu Tao* (*Six Military Strategies*), an ancient book on how to fight wisely in battles, had eight essays dedicated to the leopard strategy. Thus, the phrase leopard strategy is a synonym of military strategies. Just like the tiger pattern that marked the rank of court officials, the leopard pattern marked the rank of military officers in ancient times. In the Ming and Qing dynasties (1368-1911), military officers wore robes, namely *Buzi*, which were embroidered with the leopard pattern.

豹不但凶猛善搏，而且善于隐藏，很有"谋略"，所以它不仅代表勇猛，还是韬略的象征。古兵书《六韬》中有八篇称为"豹韬"，因此后来人们称用兵之术为"豹韬"。与虎的图案一样，豹图案在古代也是武职人员的品级标志。明、清两代，武官所穿官服的"补子"上就绣有豹的图案。

> 太平安定——象

三千多年前，黄河流域的中原地区气候湿润，森林密布，古老的中华象自由地生活在泾渭湿地。夏商时期，人与大象为伴，在中华文明的开端留下了印记。可惜的是，随着黄河流域环境的不断恶化，大象的分布范围逐渐南移，最终移到了云南西双版纳及南亚、东南亚部分地区。

象虽然身躯庞大，力气超群，但性情温顺，很早就被人类驯服。据史料记载，宋代的皇宫中设有专门饲养象的象苑，每逢祭祀大典，都会有象车游行。人们认为看见大象能带来好运，所以都前去观

> Peace and Tranquility: Elephant

Three thousand years ago, the Central Plains region of the Yellow River basin had humid climate and vast forest areas where the ancient Chinese elephant used to live freely, particularly in the wetlands of Jinghe

- 青铜象尊（商）
Bronze Elephant Statue (Shang Dynasty, 1600 B.C.-1046 B.C.)

- 上海玉佛寺影壁上的"太平有象"浮雕

象与"吉祥"的"祥"同音，瓶与"平安"的"平"同音，所以象与瓶组合成"太平有象"，喻示天下太平。

Elephant and Bottle Relievo on Screen Wall of Yufo Temple in Shanghai

The character *Xiang* (elephant) in Chinese sounds similar to the second character of *Jixiang* that means luck, while the character *Ping* (bottle) sounds the same as the first character of *Ping'an* referring to peace. Therefore, the combination of elephant and bottle can refer to peace in the world.

看，形成"御街游人嬉集，观者如织"的热闹场面。

象神态安详，行走稳健，被认为是太平盛世的象征、祥瑞之兽。《宋书·符瑞志》说："象者，

River and the Weihe River. During Xia and Shang dynasties (approx. 2070 B.C-1046 B.C.) ancient Chinese and the elephant lived together in peace and left their external footprints at the beginning of Chinese civilization. However, with the deterioration of the environment in the Yellow River basin, the distribution of the elephants gradually moved southward, and eventually moved to Xishuangbanna of Yunnan Province and some areas of South Asia and Southeast Asia.

山之精也，王者德泽流洽四境则出。"所以古代的皇宫中设有铜顶镏金宝象，帝王的陵墓处也常设有大象石雕，表达了统治者希望国家安定、政权稳固的愿望。

Although the elephant has a huge body and great strength, but it has a gentle disposition. Thus, it has long been tamed by mankind. According to historical records, there were elephant barns in the Forbidden City of the Song Dynasty (960-1279). Important ritual ceremonies would always have the elephant cart procession. As it was said that seeing elephants would bring good luck, the elephant cart procession was rather popular, forming the scene that viewers gathered happily to see the elephant in a huge number.

The elephant was considered to be an auspicious creature that symbolizes peace and prosperity due to its serene expression and steady pace. According to *Furui Zhi (Semiotical Omens)* of *Song Shu (History of the Song Dynasty)*, the elephant is the essence of mountains. It will appear when the virtue of the emperor benefits everywhere. Thus, ancient Forbidden Citys would have gilded copper statues of elephants; besides, the mausoleum of emperors would have elephant sculptures to express their hope for a stable nation and a strong regime.

- 青花朵花纹象耳瓶（明）
Blue-and-white (*Qinghua*) Porcelain Vase with Elephant Design Ears and Floral Pattern (Ming Dynasty, 1368-1644)

曹冲称象

　　曹冲（196—208）是东汉末年北方军阀曹操的儿子，从小聪明、仁爱，深受曹操喜爱。曹冲五六岁时，东吴霸主孙权送来一头巨象，曹操想知道这头象的重量，可部下都想不出称象的办法。曹冲说："把象放到大船上，在水面所达到的地方做上记号，再往船上装其他东西，使水面也到达那个记号处，最后称一下这些东西，就能知道大象的重量了。"曹操听了立刻下令照做，果然称出了大象的重量。

Cao Chong Weighing the Elephant

Cao Chong (196-208) was the son of the northern warlord Cao Cao during the late Eastern Han Dynasty. Being smart and kind-hearted, he was Cao Cao's favorite son since he was a kid. When Cao Chong was at the age of five or six, Sun Quan sent Cao Cao a giant elephant as a gift. Cao Cao wanted to know the weight of the elephant, but no one could come up with an idea. Cao Chong said: "Place the elephant on a ship and mark where the water reaches. Then, load something else on the ship until the water also reaches the same mark. Weighing how heavy these things are we can find out the weight of the elephant." On hearing this, Cao Cao immediately ordered people to do so and they got to know the weight of the elephant.

- 白玉雕大象摆件（清）
  Jade Elephant Statue (Qing Dynasty, 1616-1911)

> 瑶光清明——鹿

鹿是一种形象可爱、性情温顺的动物，四肢细长，身上有漂亮的花点，雄鹿头上还长着枝角，奔跑起来十分灵巧而优美。在中国古代传说中，鹿是一种有灵性的兽类，为北斗七星之一的瑶光星散开而生成。瑶光象征祥瑞，所以鹿也被赋予了吉祥的意义。

古人认为鹿的寿命很长，因而，鹿被看作长寿的象征。传说

- 鹿纹瓦当（战国）
Eaves Tile with Deer Pattern (Warring States Period, 475 B.C.-221 B.C.)

> Holy and Pure: Deer

Deer is a lovely and docile animal with slender limbs and beautiful dots. Bucks have antlers on their heads and run in a smart and beautiful manner. In ancient Chinese legends, deer is a spiritual creature that came from one of the stars of the Big Dipper, namely the *Yaoguang* Star. As *Yaoguang* resembles auspice, deer is entitled as a sign of auspicious meaning, too.

Ancient Chinese believed that deer's life is very long, so it is a symbol of longevity. Legend says that when the deer is 500 years old, its hairs would change to white and was known as the mythical White Deer. According to the *Furui Zhi* (*Semiotical Omens*) of *Song Shu* (*History of the Song Dynasty*), white deer will arrive when the emperor is benevolent to his subjects. Thus, deer is said to be a symbol of peace and good policy. In Taoist legends, white deer is also the mount of immortals. They often

043

瑞兽 Auspicious Animals

• **粉彩福禄寿纹盖碗（清）**

画面由蝙蝠、梅花鹿和象征长寿的寿桃组成，"蝠"与"福"、"鹿"与"禄"谐音，喻示福气、利禄、长寿三者兼而有之。

Famille Rose Lidded Bowl with Design of *Fu* (Blessing), *Lu* (Wealth) and *Shou* (Longevity) (Qing Dynasty, 1616-1911)

The pattern illustrates the Longevity Peaches, bats, and sika deer. Since in Chinese, bat is homonym of happiness and deer sounds the same as wealth, the scenes combines three meanings, including happiness, wealth and longevity.

中，鹿活到500年时，全身毛色会变为雪白，称为"白鹿"，是"神兽"。《宋书·符瑞志》中写道："白鹿，王者明惠及下则至。"鹿是天下太平、政治清明的象征。在道教传说中，白鹿还是"神仙"的坐骑，"神仙"常骑着白鹿或乘坐白鹿所驾之车来往于天地之间。

鹿有群居的特性，《诗经》中曾有"呦呦鹿鸣，食野之苹。我有嘉宾，鼓瑟吹笙"的名句，描写了朋友欢聚、宾主宴饮的热闹场面。所以后人常用"鹿鸣"来比喻朋友相聚的欢乐情景。

travel between heaven and earth by riding the white deer or in carts led by the white deer.

Deer prefers to live in herd. In *The Book of Songs*, there are famous verses: "The deer call to one another with pleased sounds, eating the wormwood of the fields. I have here admirable guests, for them we blow the bamboo organ and play the lutes. The blow shakes all the organ's tongues." It depicts a boisterous scene of friends getting together and having a great party. Therefore, people frequently used "deer cry" to describe the joy of getting together with friends.

• **青玉鹿衔灵芝纹笔架（明）**

Gray Jade Pen Rack with a Deer Holding the Glossy Ganoderma (Ming Dynasty, 1368-1644)

白鹿洞书院

白鹿洞书院位于江西庐山五老峰东南，唐德宗贞元年间，河南洛阳的学者李渤与其兄李涉在此隐居读书。李渤养有一头白鹿，白鹿温驯而颇通人性，甚至会替主人购买纸张、笔墨和生活用品，周围的乡亲都十分惊异，称李渤为"白鹿先生""白鹿山人"。后来李渤功成名就，当了江州（今江西九江）刺史，再来这里寻找白鹿，白鹿早已不见。人们传说它本是神鹿，已经返回天庭了。于是李渤在这里修建了亭台楼阁，由于这里山峰环绕，形如一洞，故取名为"白鹿洞"。五代南唐时期，"庐山国学"在这里建立；宋代初年扩建为书院，并正式定名为"白鹿洞书院"，位居全国四大书院之首。

Bailudong (White Deer Cave) Academy

Bailudong (White Deer Cave) Academy is located on the southeast side of Wulao Peak of Lushan Mountain in Jiangxi Province. Scholar Li Bo and his elder brother Li She were studying there and living an elusive life during the Zhenyuan Year of Emperor Dezong's reign of the Tang Dynasty (618-907). Li Bo raised a white deer that was docile and as intelligent as human. Sometimes, the deer even went to buy papers, ink, writing brushes and daily necessities for him. Local people were all surprised and called Li Bo "Mr. White Deer" and "White Deer's Elusive Scholar". Later, when Li Bo became a famous poet and governor of Jiangzhou (now Jiujiang of Jiangxi Province) he came back to look for the white deer, but it had gone. It was rumored that the white deer was from Heaven and it had been back. Li Bo built pavilions and houses there. As there were peaks around, the constructions seemed to be situated in a cave, and thus were named the White Deer Cave. During the Southern Tang Dynasty (937-975) of the Five dynasties, the Sinology Institute of Lushan Mountain was built there. It was expanded to an academy and was officially named *Bailudong* (White Deer Cave) Academy in the Song Dynasty (960-1279). It became the best of the top four academies throughout China at that time.

- 江西白鹿洞书院

Bailudong (White Deer Cave) Academy of Jiangxi Province

> 昌盛发达——马

家马是由野马驯化而来的，中国是最早开始驯化马匹的国家之一。山东、河南等地的大汶口文化及仰韶文化时期的遗址中，出土了不少相关遗物，都证明了早在6000多年前的中国，野马就已被驯化为家畜。

商周时期，朝廷已经开始设立专管养马的机构。当时的人将马分

> Prosperous and Flourishing: Horse

Domestic horses originated from wild horses that were domesticated in ancient times. China is among one of the first countries that tamed wild horses. A number of related artifacts, unearthed from primitive relics from cultures like Dawenkou Culture in Shandong Province and Yangshao Culture in Henan Province, demonstrate that wild horses had been tamed as a type of domestic animal as early as more than 6,000 years ago in China.

In the Shang and Zhou dynasties (1600 B.C.-256.B.C.), the imperial courts had begun to establish institutions that specialized in horse feeding. At that time, horses were divided into six categories,

- 商代墓葬的车马坑
Chariot Pit of Tombs from the Shang Dynasty (1600 B.C.-1046 B.C.)

• 镏金铜骑马俑（西汉）
Gilt Bronze Figurine on Horseback
(Western Han Dynasty, 206 B.C.-25 A.D.)

为6类，即种马、戎马（军用）、齐马（仪仗用）、道马（驿用）、田马（狩猎用）、驽马（杂役用）。传说周穆王曾经驾驭八匹骏马巡游全国。秦汉时期，马政机构已经十分完善，并且出现了大规模的马场。春秋战国时期，出现了判断良马的相马名家，还形成了各种流派。其中特别出名的秦国人孙阳，选马技术超群，被称为"伯乐"。

西汉时期，为了抵御匈奴和其他西域游牧民族的入侵，汉武帝下

namely stallion, army horse (for military purposes), orderly horse (for ceremonial purposes), road horse (for sending the post), paddy horse (for hunting) and nag (for hard laboring). According to legends, Emperor Mu of the Western Zhou Dynasty (1046 B.C.-771 B.C.) traveled around the country by harnessing eight horses. In the Qin and Han dynasties (221 B.C.-220 A.D.), horse administration institutions were quite comprehensive and huge race courses were built. In the Spring and Autumn Period (770 B.C.-476 B.C.) and the Warring States Period (475 B.C.-221 B.C.), famous judges of fine racing horses appeared and they belonged to different schools. The most famous judge was Sun Yang of the Qin Dynasty (221 B.C.-206 B.C.) who was known as Bo Le due to his superb talent in selecting racing horses.

During the Western Han Dynasty (206 B.C.-25 A.D.), in order to fight against the invasion of the Huns and other nomadic tribes in the Western Regions, Emperor Wu ordered to introduce high quality horse breed from Wusun and Dayuan to equip cavalry. Besides, over 300,000 horses were raised in the Northwest regions of China, which greatly improved the military power

• **西汉名将霍去病墓前的"马踏匈奴"石雕**

霍去病是汉武帝年间的著名军事将领，在与匈奴军的战斗中屡建战功。霍去病死后，汉武帝下令在自己的陵墓茂陵旁为他修建了陪葬墓。这件石雕战马的蹄下踏着一个手持弓箭的匈奴士兵，象征着西汉的声威和霍去病的战功。

Stone Sculpture of a Galloping Horse Treading on Hun Invaders in Front of the Tomb of Huo Qubing, a Famous General of the Western Han Dynasty (206 B.C.-25 A.D.)

Huo Qubing was a famous military commander in the regin of Emperor Wu of the Western Han Dynasty. He distinguished himself in the battles with the Hun army. After Huo died, Emperor Wu ordered to build Huo's tomb next to his own graveyard, the Mausoleum Mao. Under this stone horse sculpture, there is a Hun soldier armed with bows and arrows, symbolizing the reputation of the Western Han Dynasty and Huo's achievements in the battle.

令引进西域乌孙国和大宛国的良种马来装备汉军骑兵。汉朝还在西北地区养马30万匹，使汉军骑兵的数量和战斗力得到了极大的提升。隋唐和五代时期，骑兵在军中的地位得以确立。唐代的养马业非常兴盛，不仅对国防起了重要的作用，还进一步促进了中原与西域的文化交流。

除了在战场上驰骋，马匹还是人们运输货物的重要工具。中国古人曾经发明多种马车，明朝的工艺百科全书《天工开物》更是详细介绍了各种货运马车的构造方法。

of the Han-dynasty cavalry. In the Sui, Tang and Five dynasties (581-960), cavalry held important position in their army force. Horse raising industry was flourishing in the Tang Dynasty (618-907) and played important role not only in national defense, but also in cultural communication between the Central Plains and the Western Regions.

In addition to their role on the battlefields, horses were also used as an important tool to transport goods. Ancient Chinese had invented a variety of wagons. *Exploitation of the Works of Nature*, the book of the Ming Dynasty's engineering encyclopedia, reported

马与古人的生活息息相关，自然而然地成为人们心目中的吉祥动物。在中国的传统文化中，马成为雄健、智慧、进取、昌盛、发达的代名词。在古代，贤能的人才常有"千里马"之誉，因此马也是能力、贤才的象征。

detailed techniques about how to assemble several types of freight wagons.

Horse was closely related to daily life of ancient Chinese people and perhaps that is why the horse became an auspicious creature in people's mind. In Chinese traditional culture, the horse is synonymous with strong, intelligent,

- 《牧马图》 韩幹（唐）
Horse Herding Painted by Han Gan (Tang Dynasty, 618-907)

progressive and prosperous things. A genius was often known as swift horse. Hence, the horse is also a symbol of abilities and talents.

• 木雕奔马
Carved Wooden Running Horse

昭陵六骏

　　昭陵是唐太宗李世民的陵墓，位于陕西礼泉县城西北的九嵕山上。"昭陵六骏"是昭陵北阙前的六块骏马浮雕石刻。"六骏"的原型是唐太宗早年驰骋战场时骑过的6匹战马。相传六骏的图形设计出自唐代著名画家、工艺家阎立德和阎立本兄弟之手。这组石刻采用高浮雕表现手法雕刻而成，"六骏"分别是特勒骠、青骓、什伐赤、飒露紫、拳毛䯄和白蹄乌。这六匹骏马姿态、神情各异，线条简洁而有力，造型栩栩如生。这件作品在1914年曾被装箱准备盗运出境，其中"飒露紫""拳毛䯄"现藏于美国宾夕法尼亚大学博物馆，其余4块被截获，现陈列在西安碑林博物馆。

Six Horses of the Mausoleum Zhao

Mausoleum Zhao, the tomb of Li Shimin, Emperor Taizong of the Tang Dynasty, is located on the Jiuzong Mountain in the northwest of Liquan County, Shaanxi Province. Six Horses of Mausoleum Zhao refers to the stone relievo of six horses that were carved in the north area of the mausoleum. Prototypes of the six horses were six war horses that Emperor Taizong rode in his early years on the battlefield. It is said that famous painters and artists, Yan Lide and Yan Liben (who are brothers) of the Tang Dynasty designed the outline of the relievo. These horses were created with high relievo carving techniques. Their names were *Telebiao*, *Qingzhui*, *Shifachi*, *Saluzi*, *Quanmaogua* and *Baitiwu*. The six horses had different facial expressions and were carved with clean and powerful lines, making them lifelike. This art work was stolen to ship abroad in 1914. Therefore, *Saluzi* and *Quanmaogua* are in the museum of the University of Pennsylvania in the United States. Fortunately, the other four pieces were intercepted and are now displayed in the Xi'an Beilin Museum.

- 昭陵六骏中的"飒露紫"

Saluzi, One of the Six Horses in the Mausoleum Zhao

> 任劳任怨——牛

中国的古代文明是农耕文明，中国人借牛力进行开垦和耕种由来已久，所以中国人素来有爱牛、敬牛、拜牛的习俗。

对牛的驯化的历史，至少可以追溯到6000年前。在远古时期，牛主要被用作祭祀的祭品。为了掌管国家所有的牛在祭祀、军用等方面的用途，周代设有"牛人"一职，汉以后曾发展成为专管养牛的行政设置。河南安阳殷墟出土的商代甲

> Industriousness and Gentleness: Ox

The ancient civilization of China is a farming civilization and the Chinese people have a long history of using ox to reclaim wasteland for farming. Therefore, the Chinese people always have the custom of loving, respecting and worshiping ox.

The domestication of ox can be dated back to at least 6,000 years ago. In ancient times, ox was mainly used as sacrificial offering. In order to administer all the oxen of the country for sacrificial, military and other uses, the Zhou-dynasty government set up a position of Ox Man, which later was changed into an executive position for ox feeding after

- 青瓷牛形灯（东晋）
Ox-shaped Celadon Porcelain Lamp (Eastern Jin Dynasty, 317-420)

- **青铜牺尊（春秋）**

  牺尊是古代一类形制特殊的青铜酒器，器形为牛的造型，在背部凿口，设盖，注入美酒，用于祭祀。

  Bronze Ox-shaped *Xizun* (Wine Vessel) (Spring and Autumn Period, 770 B.C.-476 B.C.)

  Xizun is a kind of ancient bronze wine vessel with a special ox shape that the back is excavated to make a groove with cap, which is used to hold wine during sacrifice.

骨文，除了少量被刻在龟甲上，大多数被刻在牛胛骨上。

牛还有一项重要的用途是供人役使。牛车是最古老的陆地交通工具，有人认为，早在尧舜时期，牛车就已被发明。尽管由于速度较慢，牛车后来逐渐被马车取代，但在某些时期，牛车也用于缺马的地区或无须急行的驿运。东汉到魏晋时期，高级牛车出现了。牛车走起来慢而安稳，颠簸很小，扬起的尘土也少，而且车厢较大，人在里面可以自由坐卧。于是，魏晋南北朝时期牛车广泛流行，逐渐成为官员、贵族乃至皇帝的主要代步工具。元代大量搜刮民马，民间的畜力运输曾以牛为主。

对于中国这样一个农业文明古国，牛的最大价值还是体现在拉犁

the Han Dynasty (206 B.C.-220 A.D.). The oracle bone inscriptions of the Shang Dynasty (1600 B.C.-1046 B.C.) unearthed from the Yin Ruin in Anyang, Henan Province, were mostly engraved on ox shoulder blades, only a few on tortoise shells.

Ox's another important role is used for servitude by people. Oxcart is one of the oldest land transportation, which is believed to have been invented as early as the period of Yao and Shun (about 4,000 years ago). Although oxcart was gradually replaced by horse cart due to its slowness, it was still used in areas lacking horses or at posts where emergent delivery was not a must at certain times. Advanced oxcart appeared during the period from the Eastern Han Dynasty (25-220) to the Wei and Jin dynasties (220-420). The slow and steady walking

耕地上。据考证，牛耕最早出现在春秋时期。秦汉时期，牛耕得到了广泛普及。史书记载，汉代的地方官教百姓用犁耕田，使粮食产量大幅度提高。甘肃嘉峪关的魏晋时期古墓葬中出土了多块牛耕画像砖，佐证了当时河西地区使用牛耕技术已很普遍。在汉代，养牛备受重视。《风俗通义》上称，牛为"百姓所仰，为用最大，国家为之强弱也"。西汉时期淮南王刘安在《淮南子·说山训》中说："杀牛，必亡之数。"汉代官府制定了"盗牛者死"的严厉法令。牛是农耕的重要工具，进而又被当作象征五谷丰收的吉祥物。中国古代有在立春这一天鞭打泥塑春牛的习俗，人们相

- 黄釉竹节雕春牛图笔筒（清）
  Pen Container Made of Yellow Glaze Bamboo and Graved with Spring Ox (Qing Dynasty, 1616-1911)

of such oxcart jolted hard and raised little dust while its large carriage allowed people to sit and lie down freely. As a result, during the period from the Wei, Jin, Southern and Northern dynasties (220-589), oxcart widely prevailed and gradually became the main means of transport for officials, nobles, and even emperors. In the Yuan Dynasty (1206-1368), the government extorted a large number of horses from people, making ox become people's major animal labor for transportation.

　　For China, an ancient agricultural civilization, the maximum value of ox lies in plowing. According to research, ox farming first appeared in the Spring and Autumn Period (770 B.C.-476 B.C.). Ox farming was widely spread during the period from the Qin Dynasty (221 B.C.-206 B.C.) to the Han Dynasty. According to historical records, local officials taught the people to use plows for farming in the Han Dynasty, resulting in a substantial increase in grain production. Many bricks of the picture *Plowing Ox* were unearthed from the ancient tombs (Wei and Jin dynasties, 220-420) discovered in Jiayuguan City, Gansu Province, which proves that ox farming was very common in areas of the Yellow River's western

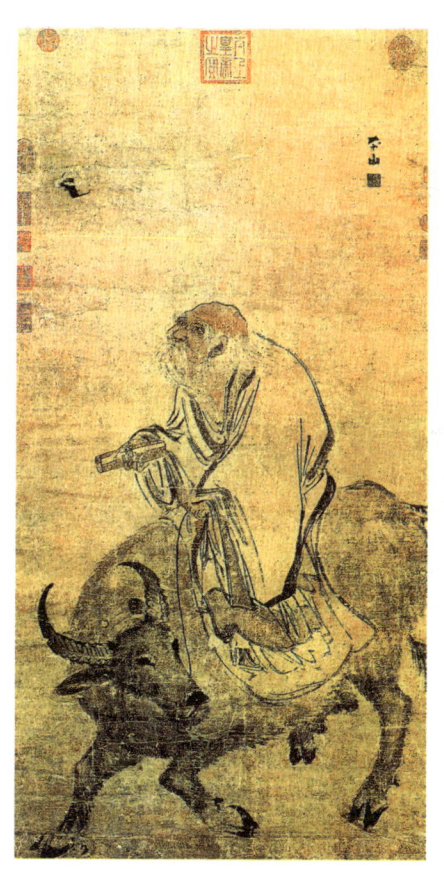

• 《老子骑牛图》 张路（明）

老子是春秋时期的思想家、道家学说的创始人。他本是东周的史官，后来周王室发生内乱，辞官离去。他骑着一头青牛到达函谷关时，被地方官关尹留住，写下了流传至今的《道德经》（又名《老子》）。

Picture of Laozi Riding Ox, by Zhang Lu (Ming Dynasty, 1368-1644)

Laozi is a thinker of the Spring and Autumn Period and the founder of Taoism. He once was a historian of the Eastern Zhou Dynasty (770 B.C.-256 B.C.) but he resigned to leave when the royal family of the Zhou Dynasty (1046 B.C.-256 B.C.) later came into unrest. When he arrived at the Hangu Pass by riding ox, a local official Guan Yin stopped him, and then he finished the *Tao Te Ching* (also known as *Laozi*), which has been spread up to now.

side at that time. Ox received great respect in the Han Dynasty. According to *Fengsu Tongyi* (*Custom Links*), oxen were respected by people and were of the most value, which could decide a country's national power. And Liu'an, Duke of Huainan in the Western Han Dynasty (206 B.C.-25 A.D.), said that anyone who killed ox would be punished to death in *Huainanzi: Lessons about Mountains*. The Han-dynasty government enacted a strict decree that the penalty for stealing ox was death. As an important tool for farming, ox was also treated as a mascot symbolizing good harvest. In ancient China, there was a custom of whipping the clay-built Spring Ox on the beginning day of spring, and people believed that this could bring a good harvest for the coming year.

Oxen were highly praised by the ancients for their spirit of industriousness and gentleness. Li Gang, a prime minister of the Southern Song Dynasty (960-1279), wrote the poem *The Sick Ox*: "While plowing lots of fields and filling lots of granaries, I've been tired out already, but on me who takes pity? If everyone is well fed with foods and lives happily at ease, I'm willing to be skinny and lie sick in the setting sun wearily." The poem vividly

北京颐和园昆明湖畔的铜牛

古人相信，将铜铸的水牛沉入水中或放置在岸边，可以起到镇水、防灾的作用。昆明湖边的这尊铜牛被铸造于清乾隆二十年（1755年），牛的背上刻有乾隆皇帝撰写的铭文。

Copper Ox by the Kunming Lake in Beijing Summer Palace

The ancients believed that submerging copper ox into water or placing it on shore could prevent flood and other disasters about water. The copper ox by the Kunming Lake was built in 1755 (20th year of Qianlong Period in the Qing Dynasty), and its back were engraved with inscriptions written by Emperor Qianlong.

信，来年可以有好的收成。

古人对牛吃苦耐劳、任劳任怨的精神十分推崇。南宋宰相李纲有《病牛》一诗："耕犁千亩实千箱，力尽筋疲谁复伤？但得众生皆得饱，不辞羸病卧残阳。"诗中将牛的艰辛和高尚描写得淋漓尽致，同时借牛言志，暗喻了自己的节操。而在古典诗词中，牛的形象常被与田园、家乡联系在一起，牛背上牧童的牧笛声总能够勾起人们对田园牧歌生活的无限向往。

describes the endurance and greatness of ox, which is also a metaphor of the writer's moral integrity by means of praising ox. In classical poetry, the image of ox is often associated with pastoral and hometown. The reed whistling played by cowherd on the back of an ox always can evoke people's infinite yearning for an idyllic life.

> 仁义吉祥——羊

羊是最早被人类驯服的家畜之一。据考古发掘，早在新石器时期，羊就已经是人类的伙伴。距今大约8000年的裴李岗文化时期出现了陶塑羊的形象，在约7000年前的河姆渡文化时期也出现了陶塑的羊。与牛、马、猪相比，羊性情温顺，更易于饲养。

> Benevolence and Auspiciousness: Sheep

Sheep is one of the earliest domesticated animals. According to archaeological excavations, sheep became human partners as early as the Neolithic Age (approx. 8000 years ago). Pottery sheep appeared in the period of Peiligang Culture dating back to about 8000 years ago as well as the period of Hemudu Culture dating back to about 7000 years

- 青铜四羊方尊（商）

四羊方尊是中国现存商代青铜器中最大的方尊，高58.6厘米，重近34.6千克。此器采用了圆雕与浮雕相结合的装饰手法，将四羊与器身巧妙地结合为一体，十分生动。

Bronze Four-sheep Rectangular Wine Vessel (Shang Dynasty, 1600 B.C.-1046 B.C.)

The four-sheep rectangular wine vessel is the largest rectangular wine vessel among the existing bronze wares of the Shang Dynasty (1600 B.C.-1046 B.C.) in China, which is 58.6 cm at height and about 34.6 kg in weight. Its decorating technique is a combination of stereoscopic and embossment carvings, combining the four sheep and the vessel's body as a whole vividly.

西北地区的古代羌族，最初就是一个以牧羊为生的民族。东汉文字学家许慎的著作《说文解字》中载："羌，西戎牧羊人也，从人从羊，羊亦声。"由于羊在羌人生活中具有重要地位，所以古代羌人以羊为图腾。

《说文解字》中还说："羊，祥也。"因为羊与"祥"同音，再加上自身利用价值很高，所以自古以来就受到人们的喜爱。汉字"美"，也是由"羊"和"大"组成的，所谓"羊大为美"。董仲舒

• 青瓷羊形器（西晋）
Celadon Porcelain Sheep Ware (Western Jin Dynasty, 265-317)

ago. They are docile in temper and easier to raise than oxen, horses or pigs.

The ancient Qiang people in the northwestern area originally were an ethnic group living on shepherds. As recorded in the book *Shuo Wen Jie Zi* (*Motivations of the Characters*) written by philologist Xu Shen in the Eastern Han Dynasty (25-220): 羌 (*Qiang*) is formed by 人 (*Ren*, human in Chinese) and 羊 (*Yang*, sheep in Chinese) in shape, and takes the pronounce of *Yang*, meaning the sheepherders in the western area. As sheep played an important role in Qiang people's lives, sheep were treated as the totem of ancient Qiang people.

The book also states that *Yang* is the same as *Xiang* (祥, auspiciousness in Chinese). Because *Yang* (sheep) has a similar pronunciation as *Xiang* (auspiciousness) in Chinese, and plus their great use value, sheep have won lots of love from the Chinese people since ancient times. In additional, the Chinese character "美" (*Mei*, beauty in Chinese) is composed by "羊" (*Yang*, sheep in Chinese) and "大" (*Da*, big in Chinese), and there is a saying that the big sheep are of beauty. Another book *Chunqiu Fanlu* written by Dong Zhongshu also says that lambs have horns but don't

• 《苏武牧羊图》 黄慎（清）
Painting of Su Wu Tending the Flock, by Huang Shen (Qing Dynasty, 1616-1911)

在《春秋繁露》里说："羔有角而不任，设备而不用，类好仁者；执之不鸣，杀之不啼，类死义者；羔食于其母，必跪而受之，类知礼者。故羊之为言犹祥与？"在董仲舒眼里，羊是知仁、知义、知礼的动物，也是仁人、君子学习的榜样。因此，中国人自古就把羊看作

attack human, and have defense but don't use them, so benevolent they are; they don't cry when being whipped, and don't whine when being killed, so righteous for death they are; when fed by their mother, they always knee to accept the milk, so courteous they are. Thus, who can say that sheep are not a representation of auspiciousness? In

- **青花瓷"三阳开泰"纹瓶（清）**

  "三阳开泰"这个说法出自中国古代的《易经》，表示春回大地、万物更新，也象征着兴旺、发达，诸事顺遂。羊与"阳"谐音，因此"三阳开泰"图案由三只羊构成。

  Blue-and-white Vase with Pattern of *Sanyang Kaitai* (Three Suns Give an Auspicious Beginning) (Qing Dynasty, 1616-1911)

  The statement of *Sanyang Kaitai*, an auspicious phrase often used to imply the illumination of golden lights and prosperity at the beginning of a year, comes from ancient China's *Book of Changes*, meaning the return of spring and the renewal of all things, as well as symbolizing prosperity and success. The character of "羊" (*Yang*, meaning sheep) is a homonym of "阳" (*Yang*, meaning sun), so the pattern of *Sanyang Kaitai* is formed by three sheep.

吉祥、美好、幸福的象征。中国南方城市广州就以羊作为城徽，并称"羊城"。

the eyes of Dong Zhongshu, sheep are animals that understand the meaning of benevolence, righteousness and courtesy, a model for good men to learn from. Therefore, sheep have been seen as a symbol of auspiciousness and happiness by the Chinese people in ancient times. The city of Guangzhou in southern China uses sheep as its emblem, and is referred to as *Yangcheng* (the Sheep City).

汉语中与羊有关的成语
Idioms Related to Sheep in Chinese

羚羊挂角
古代传说中,羚羊夜宿,将羊角挂在树上,四足离地,以避祸患。多比喻诗歌等文学作品意境超脱,不着形迹。

Antelope with Horns Hanged on Tree
The ancient legend says that when antelope sleeps at night, it will hang its horns on tree, with four feet off the ground, so as to avoid danger. The idiom is usually used as a metaphor of poetry and other literary works with unconventional artistic conception and unusual linguistic application.

歧路亡羊
歧路即岔路。丢失了羊,因岔路太多而无法寻找。比喻事物复杂多变,没有正确的方向就会误入歧途。

Lose Sheep on Forked Roads
There are so many forked roads that sheep are lost, which is a metaphor for a complex and changeable situation in which people will be lost without the right direction.

亡羊补牢
牢即关牲口的圈。羊逃跑了再去修补羊圈,还不算晚。比喻出了问题以后想办法补救,可以防止进一步的损失。

Fix the Sheepfold after Losing Sheep
It is not too late to fix the sheepfold after losing sheep, which is a metaphor that further losses can be prevented as soon as a remedy is adopted after problems arise.

顺手牵羊
比喻乘机拿走别人的东西,毫不费力。

Walk Away with Sheep
A metaphor for effortlessly taking away other people's things on the sly.

羊入虎口
羊已被老虎吃到嘴里。比喻落入险境,很难幸免。

Sheep in Tiger's Mouth
Sheep have been put into tiger's mouth, which is a metaphor for falling into danger that is difficult to escape.

> 殷实有福——猪

据科学考证，作为家畜之一的现代家猪是由生活在山林、草莽和沼泽地带的野猪驯化而来的。而中国是最早驯化猪的国家之一，早在距今7000年到距今6000年的西安半坡和浙江余姚河姆渡新石器时代遗

- 浙江余姚河姆渡遗址出土的猪纹方钵（新石器时代）
Rectangle Bowl with Pig Pattern Unearthed from Hemudu Ruin in Yuyao, Zhejiang Province (The Neolithic Age, approx. 8000 years ago)

> Be Well-off and Blissful: Pig

According to scientific research, as one of the modern livestock, pig is domesticated from wild boar living in mountains, wildernesses and swamps. China is one of the earliest countries with domesticated pigs as fossils of pig bones have been unearthed from the Neolithic ruins of Banpo in Xi'an of Shaanxi Province and Hemudu in Yuyao of Zhejiang Province, which both can be dated back to 6000-7000 years ago. Studies show that these pig bones are similar to modern domestic pigs but have significant differences with wild boar.

The Chinese character "家" (*Jia*, meaning home or family) has an origin directly related to pig, which is an associative character that first originated in oracle bone inscriptions. The present character "家" contains an upper part of "宀" (a component of Chinese characters,

• 青铜豕尊（商）
Bronze Pig Wine Vessel (Shang Dynasty, 1600 B.C.-1046 B.C.)

址中，都曾发掘出猪骨化石。经研究，这些猪骨与现代家猪相近，而与野猪已有明显的差别。

汉字"家"就与猪有着直接的渊源。"家"是会意字，最早起源于甲骨文。现在看到的"家"字上半部分为"宀"，下半部分为"豕"，"豕"即猪。猪（豕）乃"六畜"之首，无猪不成家。古代人能在屋子里养猪，表示家境殷实，有肉可食，能组成一个家庭，于是房子里有猪就成了"家"的标志。

而甲骨文中的"敢"字意为"徒手捉野猪"，是衡量人是否勇敢的标准。在唐代，因"猪"与"朱"

meaning house) and a lower part of "豕" which means pig. And pig ("豕" or "猪") is the head of the six domestic animals, so it is believed that no pig no family. In ancient times, if one could afford to raise pigs in house, his family must be a well-off one with meat for meals, and could form a new family. As a result, "家", which means a house with pig, becomes the character of family in Chinese.

The character "敢"(*Gan*, meaning brave) in oracle bone inscriptions means to catch wild boars bare-handedly, which is a measuring standard for human's braveness. In the Tang Dynasty (618-907), since the character "猪" (*Zhu*, meaning pig) was a homonym of "朱" (*Zhu*, meaning red color) and the character "蹄" (*Ti*, meaning hooves) was a homonym of "题" (*Ti*, meaning writing), people would like to make a dish of *Hongshao Zhuti* (red-braised pig hooves), for students who participated in exams, hoping them *Zhubi Timing* (names written on the pass list by a red pen, *Zhubi* means the examiner's red pen, and *Timing* means the name is written on the pass list). Pig has become the mascot of ranking the first in the imperial examination for young students.

Pig has a large head and big ears,

同音，"蹄"与"题"同音，人们往往为赶考的学子做一道"红烧猪蹄"，预祝他们"朱笔题名"。猪成了青年学子科举中第的吉祥物。

　　猪长得肥头大耳，被人们认为是富贵和福气的象征，在中国的很多地方，家中老人都会给孩子做猪头鞋，期望孩子健健康康，快乐成长。因为猪喜欢用嘴拱东西，所以中国北方一些地区的年画中绘有"肥猪拱门"的图案，人们希望肥猪给自己带来财富和幸福。由于

which is regarded as a symbol of wealth and good fortune. In many places in China, the elderly make pig-head shoes for their children, hoping that they will grow healthily. Because pigs like to arch things with their mouths, a pattern of fat pig arching the door is concluded in the New Year pictures in some areas of northern China, which means that the fat pig can bring them wealth and happiness. Since the character "猪" (*Zhu*, meaning pig) is a homonym of "诸" (*Zhu*, meaning every), there is an idiom

- **白玉猪形玉握（东汉）**
  古人认为人死时不能空手而去，而猪又是财富的象征。因而汉代时人们往往将长条圆柱形的玉雕成猪形，放在死者手中。
  White Jade Grip in Pig Shape (Eastern Han Dynasty, 25-220)
  The ancients believed that a person should not pass away empty-handed, and since pig was a symbol of wealth, people of the Han Dynasty (206 B.C.-220 A.D.) usually cut the long cylindrical jade into a slender one, which then would be carved into a pig shape and put onto the hands of the dead.

- **绿釉陶猪圈（东汉）**
  Green Glazed Pottery Pigsty (Eastern Han Dynasty, 25-220)

• "肥猪拱门"剪纸（图片提供：全景正片）
Paper-cut of Fat Pig Arching the Door

猪与"诸"谐音，所以有"诸事顺利"的意思，即任何事都能顺利完成，如愿以偿。

of *Zhushi Shunli* (诸事顺利; Here *Zhushi* means everything, and *Shunli* means going well), which means everything goes well according to people's expectations.

猪八戒

　　猪八戒是中国古典神魔小说《西游记》中的主角之一，是西去天竺取经的唐僧的二徒弟，法号"悟能"，长相与猪相似。他会变身术，能腾云驾雾，使用的兵器是九齿钉耙。猪八戒的性格中带有猪的特点，温和、憨厚、单纯，同时又有好吃懒做的缺点，是个受老百姓喜爱的喜剧人物。

Pigsy

Pigsy is one of the protagonists in the classical Chinese mythical novel *Journey to the West*, in which he is the second apprentice of Monk Tang who journeys to India for Buddhist sutras, and has a Buddhist name of Wuneng. His face similar to pig. Pigsy is able to make transfiguration and fly on clouds, and his weapon is a rake with nine teeth. His personality is similar to that of a pig, warm, simple and pure, but gluttonous and lazy, which is a comic character appealing to people.

▶ 泥塑猪八戒背媳妇
Clay Statue of Pigsy Carrying His Wife

> ## 玉兔呈祥——兔

兔子在中国文化中有着悠久的历史。中国最古老的诗歌总集《诗经·召南》中有"肃肃兔罝，椓之

- 兔形青瓷砚滴（三国）
Celadon Porcelain Water Dropper in Rabbit Shape (Three Kingdoms Period, 220-280)

> ## Nimble Gentle as White as Jade: Rabbit

Rabbit in the Chinese culture has a long history. In the oldest Chinese poetry collection *The Book of Songs: Zhao Nan*, there is a verse: "When rabbit nets are placed one by one, the stakes are tapped in tinkling." It means that people tap the stakes to drive rabbits into the nets placed. Thus it can be proved that written records about rabbits have appeared since the Pre-Qin Period (before 221 B.C.) or earlier. As recorded in *Ruiying Tu* (*Pictures of Auspicious Animals and Birds*, Song Dynasty, 960-1279), red rabbit is of great auspiciousness and white rabbit is of medium auspiciousness. At that time, if white rabbits were discovered, people would celebrate by singing and dancing, and then presented them to the court as a way of respecting the monarch and blessing the country. This was because

• **斑竹杆兔毫笔（元）**

兔毫笔就是兔毛所制的毛笔，始于战国时期。兔毫笔又有紫毫和花白之分，其中"紫毫"是用野兔背、颈部的紫黑色毛制成的，又称"箭毫"，罕见而名贵。

Chinese Writing Brush Made of Mottled Bamboo and Rabbit Hair (Yuan Dynasty, 1279-1368)

Made of rabbit hair, such Chinese writing brush first appeared during the Warring States Period (475 B.C.-221 B.C.). It can be further divided into two types of *Zi Hao* (purple hair) and *Hua Bai* (flower white). The former is made of purple-black hair on rabbit's back and neck, which is also called *Jian Hao*, very rare and precious.

丁丁"的诗句，意思是：装好张张捕兔网，敲打木桩响叮当。可见，在先秦或更早就有关于兔子的文字记录了。宋代的《瑞应图》记载："赤兔大瑞，白兔中瑞。"那时，各地的人在发现白兔之后，往往载歌载舞，献给朝廷，显示君主贤明、海内大治。古代的野兔毛色多为灰褐色，白兔极为稀少，因此它被古人认为是祥瑞的象征。

据古代神话传说，月亮里有个"广寒宫"，美丽的女仙嫦娥和

rabbits in ancient times were mostly of gray-brown color and white rabbits were extremely rare, which were considered as a symbol of auspiciousness.

According to ancient legends, there is a Moon Palace on the moon, where lives the beautiful female immortal Chang'e and a white jade rabbit which keeps making heavenly medicine with an iron rod under an osmanthus tree. Thus, the moon in ancient literature was often called as jade rabbit, rabbit ring or rabbit soul, and the shadow of the moon was called as rabbit shadow.

一只洁白的玉兔在广寒宫中相依为命，玉兔在桂花树下抱着铁杵捣药不止，因此古代文学作品常将月亮称为"玉兔""兔轮""兔魂"，称月影为"兔影"。

由于兔子性情温和，体态乖巧，动作灵敏，它在人们心目中是聪明、善良、可爱的象征，被老百姓视为吉祥之物。人们常给儿童戴兔儿帽、穿兔儿鞋，据说这样可以保佑孩子健康成长。正月十五元宵节时，人们会挂上兔儿形象的彩灯，希望可以带来吉祥。每逢中秋节，泥塑的"兔儿爷"成为最受孩子们欢迎的玩具。兔儿爷的造型为兔首人身，头戴宝盔，身穿铠甲，手持玉杵，显得威严而富有幽默感。

Due to its gentle temperament, cute posture and ingenious actions, rabbit is regarded as a symbol of smartness, kindness and loveliness as well as auspiciousness in people's minds. People often dress their children with rabbit hats or shoes, which are said to be able to protect children with a healthy growing up; during the Lantern Festival on the

- 《梧桐双兔图》 冷枚（清）
Picture of Phoenix Tree and Two Rabbits, by Leng Mei (Qing Dynasty, 1616-1911)

fifteenth day of the first month of the lunar year, people will hang lanterns with rabbit images, hoping that they can bring good fortune. During the Mid-Autumn Festival, Lord Rabbit is the favorite toy for children. The image of Lord Rabbit is a human body with a rabbit head, wearing a helmet and armor with a jade rod in hand, dignified but full of humor.

• 兔儿爷泥塑
Clay Statue of Lord Rabbit

守株待兔

"守株待兔"的典故出自战国时期的法家著作《韩非子》。宋国有个农民，他的田地中有一截树桩。一天，一只野兔飞奔而来，一头撞在树桩上，折断了脖子死了。于是，农民便放下他的农具，守在树桩旁边，希望再有一只兔子跑来撞死在他面前。结果，他当然一无所获，成了他人的笑柄。"守株待兔"这个成语经常用来形容那些不经过努力就想获得成功的人。

Waiting for Rabbits around the Stump

The allusion of waiting for rabbits around the stump comes from the Legalist book *Hanfeizi* written in the Warring States Period. A farmer in the State of Song had a stump in his farmland. One day, a galloping rabbit crashed onto the stump and died of broking its neck. The farmer then put down his farming tool and waited around the stump, hoping that another rabbit would die in the same way. Finally, he got nothing and became the laughing stock of others. This idiom is often used to describe those who want to get unexpected success without effort.

> 封侯晋爵——猴

猴为灵长目动物，与人类有着很近的亲缘关系，所以一直以来，人们对猴子都有一种特殊的亲近感。

在中原地区，虽然图腾文化表现得不是很明显，但也不难找到崇

> Promoting to Nobility: Monkey

As a kind of primates, monkey has a close genetic relationship with human, so people always have a special sense of connection with monkey.

In the Central Plains region, it is not difficult to find traces of respecting and worshiping monkey though totem culture is dilute there. Huaiyang of Henan Province, for example, has a specialty of clay toy, namely Monkey of Human Progenitor, which is a crowned monkey with solemn appearance. It is respected as the human ancestor by the locals.

The biggest feature of monkey is that it is clever, lively, cute, funny and good at imitating. *Journey to the West*, one of China's four classics, has successfully

• 河南淮阳泥塑人祖猴
Clay Statue of Monkey of Human Progenitor in Huaiyang, Henan Province

- **《猴侍水星神图》 张思恭（宋）**

这是一幅道教人物画，画中体态丰满的美妇人就是神话中的水星神。她身旁的小猴子高举石砚，姿态生动而传神。

Picture of Monkey Serving the Mercury God, by Zhang Sigong (Song Dynasty, 960-1279)
It is a figure painting about Taoist, and the buxom and beautiful woman in the picture is the Mercury God in myths. The little monkey beside her is holding an ink stone at height, lively and vividly.

猴、敬猴的痕迹。如在河南淮阳，有一种"人祖猴"泥塑玩具的特产，造型为一只头戴冠冕的猴子，表情威严、庄重，被当地人尊崇为人类始祖偶像。

猴子最大的特点是机灵、活泼，善于模仿，滑稽而可爱。中国四大古典名著之一的《西游记》就

created the image of Sun Wukong, namely the Monkey King. Sun Wukong, a monkey god transformed from stone, has far-reaching supernatural power and is able to make 72 kinds of transfigurations. He once created a tremendous uproar in the heavenly palace and was burdened under the Wuxing Mountain by Buddha as a punishment. And later, together with Pigsy and Monk Sha, he escorted Monk Tang all the way to India for Buddhist sutras by killing devils and overcoming 81 difficulties, and eventually became an immortal. In this book written by Wu Cheng'en, Sun Wukong is the incarnation of justice, courage and smartness.

In addition, since the Chinese character "猴" (*Hou*, meaning monkey)

成功塑造了美猴王孙悟空的形象。孙悟空是由石头变成的神猴，神通广大，会七十二般变化。他曾大闹天宫，被如来佛祖压在五行山下，后来与猪八戒、沙和尚一道护送唐僧去西天取经，一路斩妖除魔，历经八十一难，终成正果。在吴承恩的笔下，孙悟空成了正义、勇敢、机智的化身。

is a homonym of "侯" (Hou, meaning nobility), monkey is regarded as a symbol of promoting to nobility by ancient Chinese people. For example, the picture of *Fenghou Guayin* (here *Fenghou* means promoting to nobility, and *Guayin* means that a monkey is hanging an official seal onto a tree) is commonly seen; the picture of *Beibei Fenghou* (*Bei* means generation), on which an adult

- 美猴王孙悟空泥塑
  Clay Statue of Sun Wukong (Monkey King)

苏州狮子林的木雕"马上封侯"
Wood Carving of Monkey Riding Horse (*Mashang Fenghou*) in Lion Grove in Suzhou

此外，由于猴与"侯"谐音，被古人当作加官晋爵的象征。如常见的"封侯挂印"图，画的就是一只猴子正把官印挂在树上。"辈辈封侯"图画的是一只大猴子背着一只小猴子，取"背"与"辈"谐音，喻示辈辈做官、官运亨通。还有一种"马上封侯"图，由马和猴两种动物组成，喻示可以立刻得到升迁，受封爵位。

monkey is carrying a little monkey, an use of the homophone pair of "背" (*Bei*, meaning carrying) and "辈" (*Bei*, meaning generation), implicating that a successful official career will be passed on from generation to generation; the picture of *Mashang Fenghou* (*Ma* means horse and the compound word *Mashang* has two meanings: on the back of a horse and immediate), which contains the images of horse and monkey, implicating an immediate promotion.

朝三暮四

　　战国时期的道家著作《庄子》中记载了这样一个寓言：宋国有个养猴子的人，养了一大群猴子，而且能明白猴子们的心思。为了养猴，这个人甚至从全家的口粮里省出粮食来供给猴子们。但是，粮食还是不够吃，于是他对猴子们说："我每天早上给你们三颗橡子，晚上给你们四颗橡子，这样够吗？"猴子们一听，很生气，都跳了起来。他又说："那我早上给你们四颗，晚上给你们三颗，这样行了吧？"猴子们听后就都很满意了。后来"朝三暮四"成为一个成语，比喻人的行为反复无常。

Three in the Morning and Four in the Evening

There is an allegory in the Taoist book *Chuang Tzu* written in the Warring States Period (475 B.C.-221 B.C.). In the State of Song, there was a man who raised a crowd of monkeys and was able to understand what monkeys were thinking. In order to raise the monkeys, the man even saved his family's food for them. However, the food was not enough, so he said to the monkeys: "I will give you three acorns for each morning and four acorns for each evening. Is that OK?" Hearing this, the monkeys became angry and turbulent, and then he said again: "What about that I give you four acorns for each morning and three acorns for each evening?" And the monkeys finally were pleased with the answer. As a result, the saying of three in the morning and four in the evening becomes an idiom, which is used as a metaphor to describe human's unsteady and changeable behaviors.

> 千岁而灵——龟

龟是一种带壳的爬行动物，虽然其貌不扬，但是寿命很长，一般能达到数百年。古人根据龟寿很长这一特点，认为它阅历丰富，龟便成了原始社会先民崇拜的"神灵"动物。

山东大汶口的新石器时代文化遗址出土了龟甲21件，上有穿孔，多

- 古代占卜用的龟甲
  Tortoiseshell Used for Divination in Ancient Times

> Immortal of Longevity: Tortoise

Tortoise is a shelled reptile that has a long life of centuries in general though it does not look beautiful. As for its longevity, the ancients believed that tortoise had experienced a lot in life and had the sacred knowledge. Thus, it was regarded as an immortal animal worshiped by primitive people.

At the Neolithic Cultural Ruin of Dawenkou in Shandong Province, 21 punched tortoiseshells were unearthed, and most of them were placed on the right side of the dead's waists while some were painted with red paintings, which might be the ornaments wore by the dead during their lifetime.

Ancient Chinese astronomers divided the stars into twenty-eight Lunar Mansions, namely the Seven Lunar Mansions of Green Loong in east, the Seven Lunar Mansions of Rosefinch

被放在死者右腰旁,有的还上涂朱彩,可能是死者生前佩戴的饰物。

中国古代的天文学家把群星分为二十八宿,东方是青龙七宿,南方是朱雀七宿,西方是白虎七宿,北方是玄武七宿。汉代人把青龙、白虎、朱雀、玄武合称为"四灵"或"四神",它们的形象常出现在画像砖、瓦当、铜镜和印章上。其中"玄武"原指黑色的大龟,到了汉代变成了缠绕在一起的龟蛇形象。汉代至宋代,官印的顶端常被铸成一只龟的形状,叫作"龟纽",成为富贵和权势的象征。

龟还有一大特点,就是能背负重物,古人因此把石碑的底座雕刻为龟的形状。龟趺碑在南北朝时出现,唐代时最为盛行,直到清代仍然沿用。明代时,人们给驮碑的石龟取名叫"赑屃",还将它列为龙的九子之一。

古人出于对龟的崇拜,喜用"龟"字取名,喻示长寿。如汉朝有陈龟、朱龟;北魏有叱列伏龟。唐朝以龟为名的人更多,最著名的有音乐家李龟年和文学家陆龟蒙。在中国民间,还有养龟、玩龟的风

• 龟纽银印(汉)
Silver Seal with Tortoise Knob (Han Dynasty, 206 B.C.-220 A.D.)

in south, the Seven Lunar Mansions of White Tiger in the west, and the Seven Lunar Mansions of *Xuanwu* (an animal related to tortoise) in the north. In the Han Dynasty (206 B.C.-220 A.D.), the Green Loong, White Tiger, Rosefinch and *Xuanwu* were collectively known as the Four Sacred Animals or Four Gods, and their images appeared on painting bricks, tiles, bronze mirrors and seals. In addition, *Xuanwu* originally referred to the black tortoise and turned into the image of a tortoise intertwining with a snake in the Han Dynasty. From the Han Dynasty to the Song Dynasty (960-1279), the top of the official seal was often cast

• 青玉龟巢荷叶纹佩（金）

Gray Jade Pendant with Tortoises on Lotus Leaves Pattern (Jin Dynasty, 1115-1234)

• 龟鹤纹玉饰（元）

龟与同样象征长寿的鹤组成"龟鹤同寿""龟鹤齐龄"图案，有长寿、平安之寓意。

Jade Ornament with Pattern of Tortoises and Cranes (Yuan Dynasty, 1216-1368)

The same as tortoise, crane is also a symbol of longevity. The two of them together form the pattern of Tortoise and Crane with the Same Life, or Tortoise and Crane with the Same Age, implicating longevity and safety.

in the shape of a tortoise, called *Guiniu* (Tortoise Knob), which was a symbol of wealth and prestige.

As tortoise had another major feature of being able to carry heavy loads, the bases of monuments were carved into the shape of tortoise in ancient times. The tortoise-shaped monument base began to emerge in the Southern and Northern dynasties (420-589), prevailed in the Tang Dynasty (618-907), and was still adopted in the Qing Dynasty (1616-1911). In the Ming Dynasty (1368-1644), people named the tortoise carrying monument as *Bixi*, and listed it as one of the nine sons of loong.

As a way of respecting tortoises, the ancients liked to have their names with the character of *Gui* (tortoise), meaning longevity, such as Chen Gui and Zhu Gui in the Han Dynasty, and Chiliefu Gui in the Northern Wei Dynasty (386-534). The Tang Dynasty has more cases in point, and the most famous ones include the musician Li Guinian and the writer Lu Guimeng. Besides, raising and playing tortoises is a folk custom in China. People in southern China like to raise tortoises in yards, symbolizing longevity and health, and some of the rich even are fond of keeping mossbacks

• 北京故宫太和殿前的铜龟
Bronze Tortoise in Front of the Taihe Hall in the Forbidden City, Beijing

俗。江南人家喜欢在庭园中养龟，以象征长寿、健康，有的富庶人家还爱饲养绿毛龟，绿毛龟如同一块翡翠浸在水中，十分悦目。

(tortoises with green hair), which look like a piece of emerald submerged in the water, very pleasing to the eye.

> 飞鼠迎福——蝙蝠

> Flying Elf of Felicity: Bat

　　蝙蝠属于翼手目的哺乳动物，是哺乳类动物中唯一真正能飞的，其前后肢都有薄膜与身体相连而形成翼翅，喜在夜间活动，在飞行

Bat is a chiropteran mammal, the only mammal that is able to fly, and its fore and hind limbs contain a film connected to its body to form wings. Bat is also a nocturnal animal, which preys on

圆凳上的蝙蝠纹样
Bat Pattern on Round Stool

- 红木雕蝙蝠纹圆凳（清）
Rosewood Round Stool with Bat Pattern (Qing Dynasty, 1616-1911)

• 青花蝙蝠纹盘（清）
Blue-and-white (*Qinghua*) Porcelain Plate with Bat Pattern (Qing Dynasty, 1616-1911)

• 仁寿五福纹铜镜（清）
Bronze Mirror with Pattern of Five Bats Circle the Character Longevity (*Renshou Wufu*) (Qing Dynasty, 1616-1911)

small flying insects in flight, such as mosquitoes and moths. According to *Shuowen Jiezi* (*Motivations of the Characters*) written by Xu Shen in the Eastern Han Dynasty (25-220)—bat is the wing of clothes. Since bats look like mice, ancient legends state that bat is transformed from mouse, thus it is also known as the Flying Mouse. According to *Xiao Jing: Yuan Shenqi* (Han Dynasty, 206 B.C.-220 A.D.), a bat has a similar appearance to a mouse… and it is said that it is transformed from the mouse.

As the character "蝠" (*Fu*, meaning bat) is a homonym of "福" (*Fu*, meaning felicity), bat in China has been treated as a symbol of happiness and felicity since ancient times. Although bat does not have a beautiful appearance, the ancients have successfully utilized their imagination and different deformation techniques to beautify it into auspicious patterns of freely-curling, auspicious-clouds-like and personably-flying ones, which have become one of the most common traditional decorative patterns. The bat pattern can be used individually or jointly with other patterns. A flying bat is called *Fu Zai Yanqian* (*Fu* means felicity, and *Zaiyanqian* means

中捕食蚊、蛾等小飞虫。东汉许慎的《说文解字》中有"蝙蝠，服翼也"的记载。由于蝙蝠的外形与老鼠近似，在传说中，蝙蝠是由老鼠变化而来的，故又被称为"飞

• 福寿双全纹翡翠佩饰
Emerald Pendants with Longevity and Happiness (*Fu Shou Shuang Quan*) Pattern

鼠"。汉代的《孝经·援神契》记载，蝙蝠"形绝类鼠，……俗言老鼠所化也"。

由于"蝠"与"福"同音，蝙蝠在中国自古以来就被当作幸福、福气的象征。虽然蝙蝠的外貌并不美观，但古人运用丰富的想象力和变形手法，把蝙蝠造型美化成卷曲自如、翅展如祥云、风度翩翩的祥瑞图案，使之成为最常见的传统装饰纹样之一。蝙蝠纹样可单独构成图案，也可与其他事物共同组成图案。一只蝙蝠飞舞称"福在眼前"；蝙蝠与马组成"马上得福"；红色的蝙蝠围成一圈，被称为"洪福齐天"；五只蝙蝠与"寿"字组成"五福捧寿"。

something has come), which means the felicity has come; the combination of bat and horse is called *Mashang Defu* (*Ma* means horse and the compound word *Mashang* has two meanings: on the back of a horse and immediate; *Defu* means obtaining felicity), which means that one is obtaining felicity immediately; the red bats in a circle is called *Hongfu Qitian* (*Hong* means vast, *Qi* means the same as, and *Tian* means heaven), which means that one's vast felicity is as high as the heaven; the combination of five bats and the character "寿" (*Shou*, meaning the length of life) is called *Wufu Pengshou* (*Wu* means five and *Peng* means holding), which means that the five kinds of felicities is supporting a long life.

吉祥的鱼

鱼在新石器时代就是人类最重要的食物来源之一，而且寄托着原始先民的企盼和祈望。因为鱼能大量产子，人们把鱼奉为"神灵"，希望像鱼一样生殖力强，多子多孙。唐宋时期，贵族喜欢在身上佩戴鱼形的信符，即"鱼符"，是身份的象征。"鱼"与"余"谐音，表示富裕、美满。过年时，人们会张贴鱼的年画，合家团圆的餐桌上总少不了一条大鱼，象征年年有余、财源广进。僧尼诵经时常敲打木鱼。木鱼指被刻成鱼形的木头。据说木头只有被刻成此形状，打击的声音才会清脆、悦耳，并传播得很远。

Auspicious Fish

Fish was one of the most important sources of food in the Neolithic Age (approx. 8000 years ago), and was entrusted with the primitive people's hopes and wishes. Because of the strong reproduction ability of fish, people respected fish as gods, hoping that they would be able to have many children, just like fish. During the period from the Tang Dynasty (618-907) to the Song Dynasty (960-1279), the noble liked to wear fish-shaped token called Fish Token, which was a symbol of status. The character "鱼" (*Yu*, meaning fish) was a homonym of "余"(*Yu*, meaning the remaining), which meant abundance and prosperity. During the Chinese New Year people would post fish pictures and would have a big fish on the table for the family reunion dinner, a symbol

- 双鱼纹尖底罐（新石器时代）
V-bottom Tank with Pattern of Two Fishes (The Neolithic Age, approx. 8000 years ago)

that the family would have enough things to spend and make plenty of money in the coming year. What's more, while monks and nuns were chanting, they often knocked on wooden fish, which was woodcut in a shape of fish. It is said that only when a wood is carved in such shape, can it be knocked to make clear and sweet sound that is able to spread far away.

- 釉里红鱼纹碗（清）
Underglazed Red Porcelain Bowl with Fish Pattern (Qing Dynasty, 1616-1911)

- 五彩鱼藻纹罐（明）
Polychrome Porcelain Jar with Fish and Aquatic Plants Designs (Ming Dynasty,1368-1644)

祥禽
Auspicious Birds

　从远古时代起，中国人就开始将鸟奉为"神灵"，加以崇拜。鸟纹是早期文化遗址和夏、商、周青铜器上最常见的动物纹样。对鸟的崇拜源于原始的生殖崇拜。随着社会文化的发展，鸟在人们心目中逐渐成为自由、优美、灵巧和吉祥的象征，与瑞兽相比，祥禽体现更多的是柔美。

Chinese people have begun to respect birds as gods since ancient times, and bird patterns are the most common animal patterns in early cultural ruins and on the bronze wares of the Xia Dynasty (approx. 2070 B.C.-1600 B.C.), the Shang Dynasty (1600 B.C.-1046 B.C.) and the Zhou Dynasty (1046 B.C.-256 B.C.). The bird worship comes from the primitive phallic worship, and with the social and cultural developments, birds in people's minds gradually become the symbol of freedom, grace, smartness and auspiciousness. Compared to the auspicious animals, the auspicious birds are more of an embodiment of tenderness.

> 四海升平——凤凰

凤凰是传说中的神鸟,起源于原始社会的图腾崇拜,在新石器时代的河姆渡文化遗址中就已发现了凤纹饰品。凤凰的形象集合了鸡首、燕颔、蛇颈、鹰爪、鱼尾、龟背和孔雀翎毛,可以说是集众多动物之大成的美的化身。"凤凰"是这种"神鸟"的雌雄合称:雄鸟称"凤",雌鸟称"凰"。

- 白玉龙凤纹玉璜(战国)
White Jade *Huang* (arc-shaped article) with Loong-phoenix Pattern (Warring States Period, 475 B.C.-221 B.C.)

> The Whole World Is at Peace: Phoenix

Phoenix is a mythical bird that originated in the totemic worship of primitive societies. Ornaments with phoenix patterns have been found in the Hemudu Cultural Ruin of the Neolithic Age (approx. 8000 years ago). The image of the phoenix is a combination of a rooster's head, a swallow's jaw, a snake's neck, an eagle's talons, a fish's tail, a tortoise's back and a peacock's feather, which can be said to be the incarnation of the combining beauty of many animals. *Fenghuang* (phoenix) is the collective name of the male and female of such bird, in which *Feng* means the male and *Huang* means the female.

In ancient times, the phoenix was the symbol that the whole world is at peace. According to legends of ancient times, the Emperor Huang, who just ascended

- **青铜凤柱斝（商）**

斝为古代煮酒或温酒器，出现于夏代，流行于商代至西周时期。

Bronze *Jia* with Phoenix-shaped Pillars (Shang Dynasty, 1600 B.C.-1046 B.C.)

Jia is a kind of ancient container used to boil or warm wine, which appeared in the Xia Dynasty (approx. 2070 B.C.-1600 B.C.) and prevailed from the Shang Dynasty (1600 B.C.-1046 B.C.) to the Western Zhou Dynasty (1046 B.C.-771 B.C.).

在中国古代，凤凰是天下安定、四海升平的象征。传说在上古时代，黄帝即位后很想亲眼看看传说中的凤凰，特地去向一位睿智的老人请教。黄帝说："我即位以来，天下太平，为什么连凤凰的影子都没有看见？"老人说："现在天下尚未太平，四方强敌虎视眈

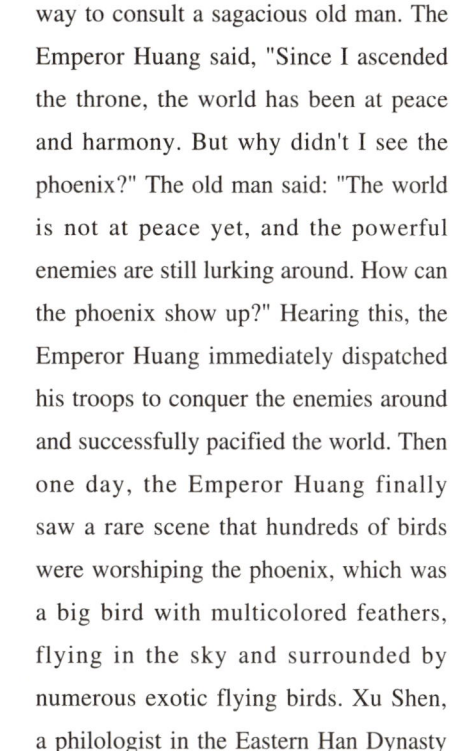

the throne, wanted to see the legendary phoenix personally and went out of his way to consult a sagacious old man. The Emperor Huang said, "Since I ascended the throne, the world has been at peace and harmony. But why didn't I see the phoenix?" The old man said: "The world is not at peace yet, and the powerful enemies are still lurking around. How can the phoenix show up?" Hearing this, the Emperor Huang immediately dispatched his troops to conquer the enemies around and successfully pacified the world. Then one day, the Emperor Huang finally saw a rare scene that hundreds of birds were worshiping the phoenix, which was a big bird with multicolored feathers, flying in the sky and surrounded by numerous exotic flying birds. Xu Shen, a philologist in the Eastern Han Dynasty (25-220), also said in his book *Shuowen Jiezi* (*Motivations of the Characters*): "Phoenix comes from the oriental kingdom of gentleman and flies to the corner of the world... it will show up when the whole world is at peace."

The Book of Songs contains a verse: "tweeting melodiously the phoenix on the high hill, growing up rapidly the phoenix tree in the morning sun." It depicts a beautiful scene that the phoenix is resting

眈，凤凰怎么可能出现呢？"黄帝听罢，马上率兵四处征讨，终于平定了天下。有一天，黄帝终于看到了难得一见的百鸟朝凤奇景：一只长有五彩翎毛的大鸟在天空中翱翔，而数不清的奇珍异鸟围着它翩翩起舞。汉代文字学家许慎也曾在《说文解字》中说凤凰"出于东方君子之国，翱翔四海之外……见则天下大安宁"。

《诗经》中有"凤凰鸣矣，于彼高冈。梧桐生矣，于彼朝阳"的句

on the phoenix tree and tweeting to the nascent sunrise in the east. According to legends, phoenix is an arrogant mythical bird, which rests only on the phoenix tree, eats only the bamboo food and drinks only the sweet water. And it is very fond of sunlight and flame. The ancient tiles, painting stones and jade carvings contain many patterns of Red Phoenix Facing to the Sun, reflecting ancient people's opinion that phoenix and the sun have a mutual dependent and corresponding relationship that phoenix can call on, fly toward and even carry the sun. Since the

- 珐琅彩龙凤纹双联瓷瓶（清）
Enamel-color Porcelain Duplex Bottle with Loong-phoenix Pattern (Qing Dynasty, 1616-1911)

- 古代婚礼必备的龙凤烛
Loong-phoenix Candles, Necessary for Ancient Weddings

• 古建筑上的凤栖梧桐图案彩画
Ancient Building's Color Painting with Pattern of Phoenix Resting on Phoenix Tree

子，描绘了凤凰栖于梧桐树上，面向东方初生的朝阳放声鸣叫的美丽画面。传说凤凰是一种孤高的"神鸟"，非梧桐不栖，非竹子的果实不食，非甜美如醴的泉水不饮。而且它非常喜爱阳光和火焰。古代瓦当、画像石和玉雕上有很多"丹凤朝阳"的图案。在古人眼里，凤和太阳是彼此依存、对应的关系，凤凰呼唤太阳、飞向太阳，甚至驮载着太阳，成为人们心目中的太阳鸟。古人常常把太阳与火看成一回事，所以凤凰又有"火鸟""火精"之称。

ancients often treated the sun and fire as one thing, so phoenix is also called the Firebird or Fire Spirit.

Since the Neolithic Age, the two auspicious animals of phoenix and loong have appeared in pair. In the Yangshao Cultural Ruin in Baoji of Shaanxi Province, a painted pottery bottle with patterns of loong and phoenix was unearthed, which dated back to seven or eight thousand years ago. The loong likes water and is fond of flying, which is changeable and dignified; while the phoenix likes fire and always faces the sun, which is unsullied and elegant. Their

从新石器时代起，龙和凤这两种祥瑞动物就开始成对出现。陕西宝鸡的仰韶文化遗址曾出土一件龙凤纹彩陶瓶，距今已有七八千年之久。龙喜水、好飞、善变、威严，而凤喜火、向阳、尚洁、高雅，它们的"神性"对应而互补，一个是众兽之君，一个是百鸟之王，两者结合，带来一派祥和之气。远古时，凤的地位高于龙，在出土的战国文物，如楚国一些龙凤图案的壁画、帛画中，展翅飞翔的凤占主导地位。但随着封建帝制的发展，龙逐渐成为帝王的象征，凤则降到附属位置，成为皇后、嫔妃等皇室

divinities are in a corresponding and complementary relation that one is the king of all animals and the other is the king of all birds, so their combination can bring auspiciousness and harmony. In ancient times, the phoenix had a higher status than the loong. Among the unearthed relics of the Warring States Period (475 B.C.-221 B.C.), flying phoenixes are the dominant patterns, such as in some of the murals and silk paintings with patterns of loongs and phoenixes of the State of Chu. However, with the development of the feudal monarchy, the loong gradually became the symbol of emperor while the phoenix was reduced to a subsidiary position representing royal or aristocratic women like queen or concubines. For example, the queen's coronet was called the Phoenix Coronet, the carriage for the queen's travelling was called the Phoenix Carriage, and the queen's body was called the Phoenix Body. The Phoenix originally was divided into male

- 青花双凤纹盘（明）
Blue-and-white (*Qinghua*) Porcelain Plate with Two Phoenixes (Ming Dynasty, 1368-1644)

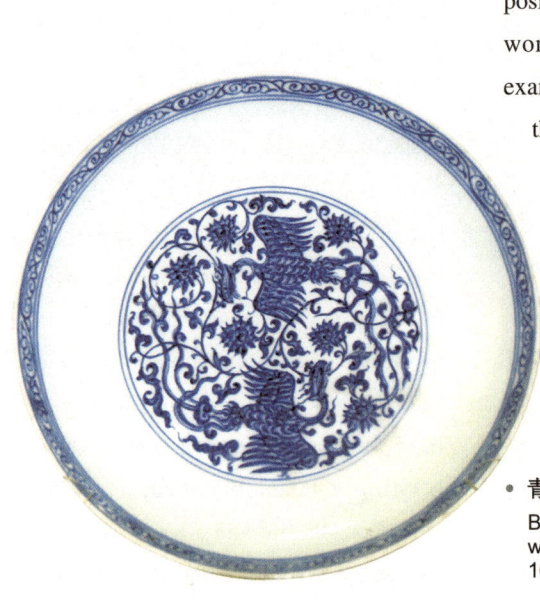

- **明定陵出土的孝端皇后凤冠**

  这件凤冠上饰有三条金龙,是以金丝堆累工艺焊接的,呈镂空状,富有立体感;两只凤以翠鸟毛粘贴而成,色彩经久艳丽。冠上还饰有红、蓝宝石一百多块,大、小珍珠五千余颗。

  Queen Xiaoduan Phoenix Coronet Unearthed in the Ding Tomb (Ming Dynasty, 1368-1644)

  This phoenix coronet is decorated with three golden loongs, which are made of superimposed spun gold welded in a hollow and stereoscopic form; the two phoenixes are made of kingfisher feather with perishable and bright colors. The coronet is also decorated with over a hundred rubies and sapphires, as well as about five thousand pearls in different sizes.

贵族女性的象征。如皇后的冠称"凤冠",皇后出行乘坐的是"凤辇",皇后的身体则称"凤体",等等。原本凤凰是分雌雄的,但在与象征帝王的龙形成对应之后,凤的形象开始逐渐不分性别,整体变得阴柔而优美,婀娜多姿。

and female ones, but after it was paired with loong that symbolizing the emperor, the image of phoenix began to desalt the difference of gender and gradually contained the features of feminine beauty and grace.

> 仙游长寿——鹤

鹤是中国特有的珍禽，包括丹顶鹤、灰鹤、蓑羽鹤等多种，但在传统文化中，最受重视的要数历来被视为"羽族之长"的丹顶鹤。丹顶鹤身披白色羽毛，头顶有一小块红色，颜色鲜艳，与洁白的羽毛相互映衬，显得格外鲜艳，深得历代文人的赞誉。

> Traveling Immortal with Long Life: Crane

Crane is a kind of unique Chinese rare bird, and its varieties include the red-crowned crane, grey crane, demoiselle crane and so on, among which the red-crowned crane is the most important in the traditional culture and has always been regarded as the Head of Birds. The red-crowned crane has white feather and a small red patch on the head, which

- 《瑞鹤图》 赵佶（北宋）
Picture of Auspicious Cranes, by Zhao Ji (Northern Song Dynasty, 960-1127)

• 透雕"松鹤长春"【局部】

鹤在中国古代被视作"仙禽"，长颈、素羽、丹顶，传说其寿可至千年，因而被古人视为长寿鸟。

The Openwork of Cranes Playing among Evergreen Pine Trees [Part]

The crane is regarded as an immortal animal in ancient China. It has a long neck, plain-colored feathers and a red crown. Legend says it can live for 1,000 years and was viewed as a long-living bird by the ancient Chinese.

《诗经》中就有《鹤鸣》一章，描述了鹤栖息于野草之中，善于鸣叫，用以比喻隐居山野而品德高尚的贤能之人教诲统治者重用他们。这是鹤的艺术形象最早在古文献中出现。鹤形体修长，举止优雅，叫声清脆，被古人看作超凡脱俗的"仙禽"。明清时期，鹤不仅被饲养于皇家园林

looks like a bright red drop with a great contrast against the white feather, creating an extraordinarily brilliant feature and winning lots of praise from writers of all ages.

In *The Book of Songs*, there is a chapter named *Crane's Tweeting* depicting that a crane rested in the weeds and was good at tweeting, which was used as a metaphor that the reclusive but virtuous sages were teaching the rulers that they should be put into important positions. This is the earliest artistic image of the crane in ancient literature. Because of its slender body, elegant behavior and clear tweeting, the crane was seen as a unique immortal bird by the ancients. During the period from the Ming Dynasty (1368-1644) to the Qing

• 缂丝团鹤纹一品夫人袍服（清）

明清时期的官员分为九品，最高等级称为"一品"。一品文官的官服上绣有仙鹤图案，所以鹤又称"一品鸟"。这件袍服是清代受册封的一品官员夫人最隆重的礼服，前后衣襟、肩、袖上共饰有9个团形云鹤图案，工艺极其精美。

Robe for the Wife of the First-grade Official with Waving Embroidered Pattern of Crane Groups (Qing Dynasty, 1616-1911)

Officials of the Ming Dynasty and the Qing Dynasty are divided into nine grades and the highest grade is called First Grade. The robes of the first-grade civilian officials are embroidered with crane patterns, so crane is also known as the First-grade Bird. This robe is the most solemn dress for the wife of the first-grade official entitled by the Qing government, which is decorated with a total of 9 patterns of cloud-like crane groups on the front and rear skirts, shoulder and sleeves thought refined process.

之中，而且皇宫殿堂和园林中也开始广泛出现鹤的造型和图案。清代更将一品文官官服上的图案定为仙鹤，将鹤的地位提到仅次于龙和凤的高度。

鹤的寿命一般为五六十年，在禽类中比较长寿，而古人认为其寿命更为长久。西汉时期的著作《淮南子》中说："鹤寿千岁，以极其游。"再加上鹤体羽洁白，使人联想到老人的满头银发，因此被人们视为吉祥和长寿的象征。人们常用"鹤发童颜"来形容精神矍铄的长寿老人。

Dynasty (1616-1911), the crane was housed in royal gardens, and the palace halls and gardens also began to use crane's shape and pattern as decoration widely. The Qing-dynasty government even printed the robes of the first-grade civilian officials with the pattern of cranes, raising the crane's status to a degree only second to loong and phoenix.

Cranes generally can live for fifty or sixty years, which is a long life for birds. However, the ancients believed that it could have a longer life. For example, *Huai Nan Zi*, a book of the Western Han Dynasty (206 B.C.-25 A.D.), states that the crane has a long life of a thousand years and can fly to anywhere. In addition, crane's white feather can remind people of the silver hair of the elderly, so it is regarded as a symbol of auspiciousness and longevity. People often use the idiom of Crane Hair and Child Face to describe vigorous and long-lived seniors.

- 黄玉雕仙鹤捧桃寿星（清）
  Topaz Carving of Immoral Crane and God of Longevity Holding a Peach (Qing Dynasty, 1616-1911)

梅妻鹤子的林和靖

林逋（967—1028），宋代著名诗人，钱塘（今浙江杭州）人，世称"和靖先生"。他自幼好学，通晓经史，性孤高、自好，成年后隐居在杭州西湖。相传他一生没有出来做官，也没有娶妻、生子，平时就喜欢遍交文士、僧人，过着"仙人"一般的日子。他最爱植梅和养鹤，自谓"以梅为妻，以鹤为子"。他在家中养了两只仙鹤，打开笼门，它们就会飞入云霄，在空中盘旋，然后再回到笼里。林逋常常驾着小舟在西湖游荡，有客人到家中拜访时，家里的小童就会先把客人请进来坐，然后打开笼子放出仙鹤。过一会儿，林逋看到仙鹤飞天，就会驾着小舟回家。

Lin Hejing Who Looked upon Plum Blossom as Wife and Crane as Children

Lin Bu (967-1028), a famous poet of the Song Dynasty (960-1279), was born in Qiantang (present Hangzhou of Zhejiang Province) and was commonly called Mr. Hejing. He had been studious and proficient in the classics and history since his childhood, but he was also an arrogant and unsocial man who was secluded to the West Lake in Hangzhou after growing up. It was said that he had never come out to secure an official position in his lifetime, and never got married nor had children, and what he liked was making friends with literates and monks, living a life like immortals. His favorite hobby was raising plum blossoms and cranes, and he claimed that "plum blossom is my wife and crane is my child". He raised two cranes at his home, and if their cage was open, they would fly up into clouds, hover in the air and fly back to the cage again. Lin Bu often boated on the West Lake, and if there was a visitor, his servant would lead the visitor home and open the crane cage to release the cranes. After a while, Lin Bu would boat back home when he saw his cranes flying in the sky.

《梅妻鹤子》 潘振镛（近代）
Plum Blossom Wife and Crane Children, by Pan Zhenyong (Modern Times)

> 富贵有情——孔雀

除了神话中的凤凰,孔雀可以算得上自然界中最绚丽的鸟类了。"孔"在古文中是"大"的意思,孔雀就是"大鸟",它们体长为1—2米,的确是鸟中的"巨人"。雄孔雀羽毛绮丽而华美,头上一簇冠羽

- 青白玉双孔雀图玉饰(宋)
Greenish White Jade Ornament with Two Peacocks (Song Dynasty, 960-1279)

> Fortune and Affection: Peacock

Apart from the mythical phoenix, *Kongque* (peacock) can be regarded as the most colorful bird in nature. *Kong* means big in ancient Chinese, so *Kongque* (peacock) means a big bird with a body about 1-2 meters long, which indeed is the giant among birds. Male peacock has beautiful and gorgeous feathers: its head is towered with a crest; its back and wings are covered with russet, blue-black and verdant colors; and the long tail is twice the length of its body, which looks flowery and colorful in the sunshine. The peacock's tail usually is closed and dragged behind the body, but if it opens, you will think that you are looking at a huge piece of bright brocade.

Because of its colorfulness, the peacock was called as the Pattern Bird by the ancients, meaning the bird with beautiful patterns. *Shang Shu: Book of*

• 绿釉孔雀陶灯（汉）
Green Glazed Pottery Peacock Lamp (Han Dynasty, 206 B.C.-25 A.D.)

高高耸立，背部和翅膀上覆盖着黄褐、青黑、翠绿的羽毛，而长长的尾羽是身长的两倍，在阳光的照耀下显得华丽多彩。平时，孔雀的尾羽合拢并拖在身后，开屏时犹如鲜艳的锦缎。

孔雀因其色彩斑斓，被古人称为"文禽"，即花纹漂亮的鸟。《尚书·周书》中写道："成王

Zhou once stated that during the Period of Emperor Cheng (1042 B.C.-1021 B.C.), the westerners presented peacocks as a tribute. This is the earliest historical records about peacock.

As an auspicious bird, the peacock is seen as a symbol of official rank and power. During the period from the Ming Dynasty (1368-1644) to the Qing Dynasty (1616-1911), the robes of the second-grade and third-grade civilian officials were tapestried with peacock patterns. In the Qing Dynasty, the rear part of official's hats was added with a Flower Plume (a kind of feather ornament) made of the peacock's tail and the grades of official rank were distinguished by the Plume Eye, which referred to the eye-like stripes on the tip of plumes. A Flower Plume may have one, two or three Plume Eyes, and those with three Plume Eyes were the most valuable ones, which could only be worn by *Beizi* (a title for nobility) canonized by the emperor. Later, the peacock or Flower Plume also became the mascot for a successful official career.

According to *New Book of Tang*, when the wife of Li Yuan, the founding emperor of the Tang Dynasty (618-907), was young, her father Dou Yi wanted

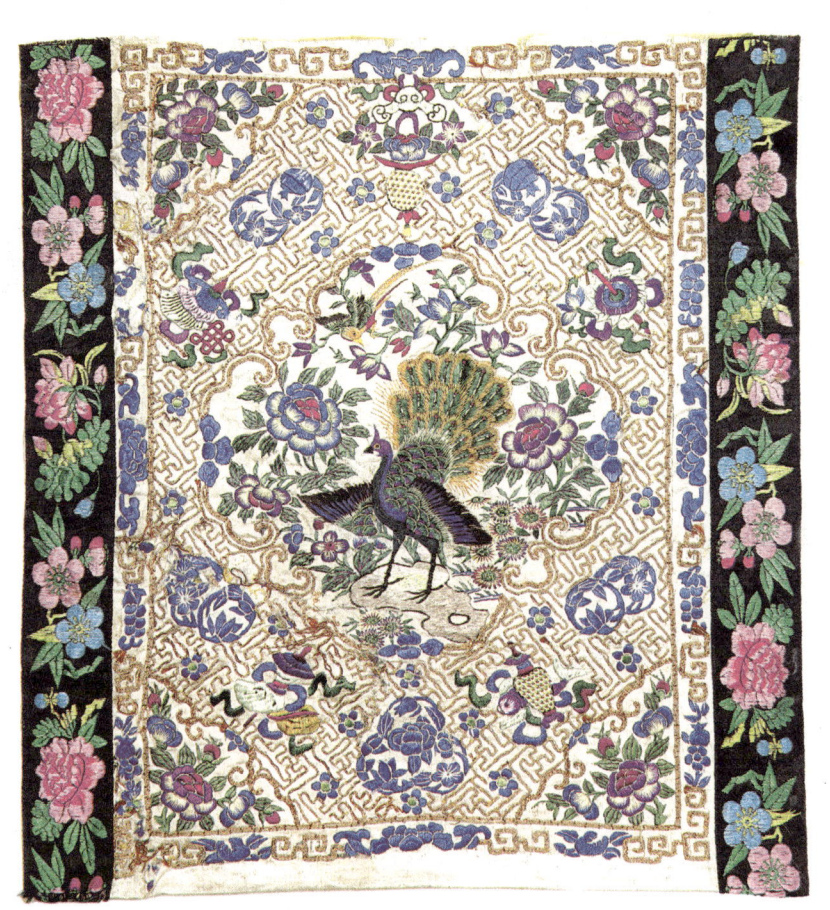

• 孔雀开屏图案绣品（清）
Embroidery with Pattern of Peacock Spreading Tail (Qing Dynasty, 1616-1911)

时，西方人献孔雀。"这是关于孔雀的历史记载。孔雀美丽的羽毛历来是人们喜爱的装饰品。

孔雀作为吉祥之鸟，还被视为官阶和权势的象征。明清时期，二品、三品文官的官服上就有孔雀图

to select a husband for his daughter and then he painted two peacocks on the door screen, allowing each suitor to shoot two arrows and promising that the one who shot on the eyes of the peacocks would be selected as the husband of his daughter. Finally, Li Yuan had his two shoots

案。清代时，官员的官帽后面装有孔雀尾羽制成的花翎，以翎眼的多少来区分官阶等级。"翎眼"指翎毛尾梢上形如眼睛的彩色斑纹。花翎有一眼、二眼、三眼之分，以三眼为最尊贵，只有皇帝册封的贝子才可佩戴。后来，孔雀或花翎还成为祈祝官运亨通的吉祥物。

据《新唐书》记载，唐代开国皇帝李渊的妻子年轻时，她的父亲窦毅为女择婿，在门屏上画了两只孔雀，令前来求婚者每人射两支箭，说射中雀目的人可中选。结果李渊两箭各中一目，成为窦家的女婿。后来人们就用"雀屏"来比喻选得佳婿。孔雀也成了爱情的象征，喻示喜结连理，姻缘天作。

- **清代官员的官帽**
  Official Hat of the Qing Dynasty

right on the two eyes of the peacock respectively and became the son-in-law of Dou Yi. From then on, people began to use Peacock Screen as a metaphor for obtaining a good son-in-law and peacock became a symbol of love and good marriage.

> 恩爱忠贞——鸳鸯

鸳鸯是一种美丽的水鸟，形体小于野鸭，栖息于山地附近的溪流、河谷、湖泊、芦苇塘等地方，以鱼虾、昆虫、野果、稻谷为食。

> Love and Loyalty: Mandarin Duck

Mandarin duck is a kind of beautiful water bird with a body smaller than wild ducks and inhabits in the near streams, valleys, lakes, reed ponds and other places in mountain region by

- 古建筑木雕"鸳鸯戏水"
  Woodcarving of Mandarin Ducks Swimming in the Pond Pattern on Ancient Building

- 鸳鸯纽铜炉（清）
Copper Stove with Mandarin Duck Knobs (Qing Dynasty, 1616-1911)

- 青花矾红描金牡丹鸳鸯纹盘（清）
Celadon Plate with Vitriol-red and Gold-traced Patterns of Peonies and Mandarin Ducks (Qing Dynasty, 1616-1911)

鸳鸯不仅会游泳，而且飞翔能力也很强，是一种候鸟，一般春季在内蒙古东北部、东北地区北部和中部繁殖，秋季则南迁到长江中下游及

eating fishes, insects, wild fruits and grains. Mandarin duck not only can swim but also has a strong ability to fly. As a migratory bird, it generally breeds in northeastern Inner Mongolia and the northern and central parts of the northeastern China in spring, and then migrates southward to the middle and lower reaches of the Yangtze River and the southeast coast area of southeast China for wintering in autumn. People think that if one of the mandarin ducks in a pair dies, the other one would never look for a new spouse again and would spend the rest of its life alone. As a result, mandarin ducks have been seen as a symbol of affectionate and loyal couples. Lu Zhaolin, who was called one of the Four Outstanding Poets of the Early Tang Dynasty, once said in his poem: "Being able to stay together with my beloved forever, even death is worthwhile; I would like to be a mandarin duck and will not envy the immortal." In the eyes of Lu, being able to stay together with the beloved forever like mandarin ducks is a happier life than being an immortal. Today, wedding stuffs are often painted with mandarin duck patterns, implicating that the newlyweds will love each other forever like mandarin ducks.

东南沿海一带越冬。人们认为，如果一对鸳鸯中的一只遭遇了不幸，另一只也不再寻觅新的配偶，而是孤独地度过余生。所以自古以来人们就把鸳鸯看作夫妻恩爱、爱情忠贞的象征。被称为"初唐四杰"之一的唐代诗人卢照邻曾在诗中写道："得成比目何辞死，愿作鸳鸯不羡仙。"在他看来，像鸳鸯一样厮守终身，赛过"神仙"的自由自在。时至今日，新婚用品上常绘有鸳鸯图案，喻示新婚夫妇像鸳鸯一样，彼此恩爱一生。

- 《鸳鸯并莲图》 齐白石（近代）
  Picture of Mandarin Ducks and Lotus Bloom on the Same Stalk, by Qi Baishi (Modern Times)

> 恋家报春——燕子

燕子在中国古代被称为"玄鸟",它体型小巧,两翅尖而长,尾羽平展时呈叉状,在飞行中捕食昆虫。燕子喜欢在民居的房梁上或墙角处筑巢,它们每年秋天迁徙到南方过冬,第二年春天会飞回之前在北方的窝里,是一种十分恋家的鸟。早在几千年前,中国人就知道燕子秋去春回的迁徙规律。燕子一般在夜里飞行,尤其在风清月朗时,飞得很快、很高;白天则在地面上休息、觅食。

而人们乐于让燕子在自己的房檐下筑巢,生儿育女,并认为这是吉祥、有福的事。就算燕子啄泥筑窝弄脏了门前的地面,人们也并不在意。燕子每逢春天从南方飞来,又被看作报春的鸟,预示春回大地,一切生机再现。唐代大诗人白居易曾在诗

> Homelover and Spring Herald: Swallow

Swallow in ancient China was known as the Black Bird, which has a compact body, two long-pointed wings and a tail looking like a fork when opened. Swallow preys on insects in flight and likes to make nests on the beam or corner of dwelling houses. It migrates southward for wintering every autumn and flies back to its previous nest in the north during the spring of the second year, which means that it is a very nostalgic bird. As early as thousands of years ago, the Chinese people realized swallow's migrating rule of leaving in autumn and coming back in spring. Swallow generally takes its migration at night and flies especially fast and high on the cool night with a bright moon, while in the daytime it always rests on the ground for foraging.

People are happy to let swallows nest and live under the eaves of their

- **北京颐和园长廊彩画"双燕图"**

  这是一幅由两只燕子组成的"双燕图"。两只燕子一雄、一雌，成双成对，象征着真诚、美好的爱情，寄托着人们希望像燕子一样夫妻恩爱、家庭美满的愿望。

  Color Painting of Swallow Pair on the Long Corridor in Summer Palace, Beijing

  The Painting of Swallow Pair consists of a male swallow and a female swallow in pair, which symbolizes the royal and wonderful love, and is entrusted with people's expectation that couples will love each other forever and have a happy family.

中写道："几处早莺争暖树，谁家新燕啄春泥。"描述了早春时节黄莺争抢树枝搭窝，而归来的燕子啄取春泥筑巢的情景。

在中国古代，科举考试的最高级别——殿试一般在杏花盛开的春天举行。殿试考中的人，皇帝会亲自设宴款待。因为宴会的"宴"与

houses and believe that it can bring good fortune. And people will not mind even if swallows stain the ground in front of the doors when they peck clay to make nests. Since the swallow comes back from the south every spring, it is seen as the bird heralding the spring, which indicates that the spring is coming back and everything is to have a new life. Bai Juyi, a famous

• 传统沙燕风筝

沙燕是北京地区的传统风筝样式，取材于展翅高飞的小燕子形象。在造型上强化了燕子展翅的动态，又使之符合风筝的结构和科学原理。其装饰图案夸张地表现了眼睛和爪子的形状，具有浓厚的民族特色和装饰性。

Traditional Swallow-shaped Kite

Swallow-shaped kite is a traditional style of kite in Beijing area. The design draws inspiration from a flying swallow and the stretching wings of the kite are exaggerated to reflect the power of the wings and elegance of the scissors-shaped tail. The decoration of swallow-shaped kite highlights the eyes and claws, and looks very exotic and entertaining.

poet of the Tang Dynasty (618-907), once said in his poem: "Somewhere the oriole birds are scrambling for the warm tree in the morning; in whose house the new swallows are pecking the spring clay." It depicts a scene that the oriole birds are scrambling for tree branches to make nests while the newly-returned swallows are pecking clay to make nets too during the early spring season.

In ancient China, the Palace Examination, the highest level of the imperial examinations, usually was held in spring time when almond blossoms were in full bloom. As the examiner of the Palace Examination, the emperor would host a banquet personally because the character "燕" (*Yan*, meaning swallow) was a homonym of "宴" (*Yan*, meaning banquet) and the pattern of Almond Grove and Spring Swallows, depicting a scene of swallows flying among almond trees, had the implied meaning of a smooth examination, a successful result and a promising career. Because male and female swallows always fly and nest in pair, so they are

"燕"谐音,所以群燕在杏树间穿梭的"杏林春燕"图案有祝愿学子科考顺利、金榜题名、前途远大的寓意。因为雌、雄燕子双宿、双飞,共同筑巢,所以人们以燕子象征爱情,用"燕侣""燕俦"比喻夫妻幸福、和谐,婚姻美满。

also regarded as a symbol of love. For example, Swallow Couple and Swallow Pair are used as a metaphor of happy couple and harmonious marriage.

• 《杂画册之四——杏花春燕》 朱耷(清)
Album of Paintings IV: Almond Blossoms and Spring Swallows, by Zhu Da (Qing Dynasty, 1616-1911)

> 灵禽兆喜——喜鹊

喜鹊又名"鹊",是一种在中国十分常见的鸟类,无论在山区、荒野、农田还是在城市,都能看到它们的身影。喜鹊是与人类最亲近的鸟类之一,通常喜欢把巢筑在民宅旁的大树上。人类活动越多的地方,喜鹊种群的数量往往也越多。古人观察到,喜鹊厌恶阴湿的气候,喜欢晴天,天气晴朗、干燥时就会欢快地跳跃、鸣叫。《易卦》说:"鹊为阳鸟,先物而动,先时而应。"古人认为,喜鹊能够在事情未发生时知其预兆,包括预报天气。

周代师旷所著的《禽经》中有"灵鹊兆喜"的记载。到了汉代,人们已经习惯了将喜鹊鸣叫看作好事将至的预兆。唐代人张鷟编写的《朝野佥载》中有这样一则逸闻:

> Sacred Bird Predicting Happiness: Magpie

Xique (magpie), also known as *Que*, is a very common bird in China, and its traces pervade mountains, wilderness, farmlands and even cities. Magpie is very close to humans and generally likes to nest on the trees next to dwelling houses. The more human activities there are, the larger magpie population there will be. The ancients have found that the magpie doesn't like damp climate but likes sunny days, and a dry and sunny day will make it jump and tweet happily. As stated in *Yi Gua*: "Magpie is a sun bird, which has feelings and makes a movement before something changes." The ancients believed that magpie has the ability to predict what will happen and react in advance, including weather forecasting.

The Book of Birds, written by Shi Kuang in the Zhou Dynasty (1046 B.C.-

- 黄地粉彩"喜鹊登梅"纹碗（清）

  "喜上眉梢"的原意是喜悦的心情从眉眼上表现出来。人们以梅花谐音"眉"字，构成喜鹊飞上梅枝的图案，喻示喜事来临，喜从天降。

Yellow Background Powder Enamel Bowl with Pattern of Magpie Flying upon Plum Tree (Qing Dynasty, 1616-1911)

The idiom *Xishang Meishao* (*Xi* means magpie or happy mood, *Shang* means on, and *Meishao* means the tips of the brows) has a meaning that the happy mood is shown on the tips of the brows. As the character "梅" (*Mei*, meaning plum) is a homonym of "眉" (*Mei*, meaning brows), the pattern of a magpie flying upon plum tree has an implied meaning that the happy things are coming.

唐朝初年，有个叫黎景逸的人，家门前的树上有个喜鹊窝，他常给巢里的喜鹊喂食，与鸟产生了感情。后来，黎景逸被人冤枉，进了监狱。有一天，那只喜鹊在他的牢房的窗前欢叫不停，很快，冤情得以昭雪，他终于平安出狱。人们更加相信喜鹊是预报喜事的吉祥之鸟。

256 B.C.), records that the sacred magpie can predict happiness. By the Han Dynasty (206 B.C.-220 A.D.), people had become accustomed to seeing magpie's chirping as a harbinger of the coming good things. *Chaoye Qianzai (Anecdotes in the Court and the Commonalty)*, compiled by Zhang Zhuo in the Tang Dynasty (618-907), contains an anecdote like this: In the early Tang Dynasty, there

was a man named Li Jingyi, in front of whose house there was a tree nested by a magpie. Li often fed the magpie and kept a good relationship with it. Later, Li was wrongly accused and was put into prison. One day, the magpie chirped happily in front of the window of his cell, and he was exonerated soon and was safely released from prison. As a result, people further believed that magpie was an auspicious bird that could predict happiness.

According to folklores, on the seventh day of the seventh lunar month, magpies will fly to the sky and form a magpie bridge on the Milky Way, allowing Niulang and Zhinü, a couple separated by the Milky Way, to meet each other. Therefore, the magpie bridge is regarded as a symbol of the marriage between men and women. In addition,

- 《喜鹊图》 齐白石（近代）
Picture of Magpie, by Qi Baishi (Modern Times)

• 古代建筑上的木雕"喜鹊牡丹"图
Woodcarving with Patterns of Magpies and Peonies on Ancient Building

在民间传说中,每年的农历七月七日,喜鹊都会飞到天上,在天河上搭起一座鹊桥,使分隔在天河两岸的夫妻牛郎和织女得以相会,所以鹊桥被认为是男女姻缘的象征。民间也常以喜鹊象征喜庆之事,举办婚礼时,人们最喜欢用喜鹊纹样的剪纸来装饰新房。

the magpie is seen as a symbol of happy things by people. When there is a wedding, for example, people always like to use the paper-cut with magpie pattern to decorate the room of the new couple.

牛郎、织女鹊桥相会

　　牛郎、织女是中国神话故事中的人物。据说牛郎从小就没了父母,哥嫂与他分家,并霸占了大部分家产,只分给牛郎一头老牛。牛郎在山上搭了一间草屋,与老牛相依为命。有一天,老牛突然开口说话,让牛郎去山的另一侧的湖边,说那里有一群仙女在洗澡,它让牛郎藏起一件红色的仙衣。牛郎按照老牛的指示,结识了红色仙衣的主人,即织女。后来织女与牛郎结为夫妻,并生了一对儿女。王母娘娘知道此事后,马上派天兵、天将捉拿织女问罪。牛郎在老牛的帮助下,披上牛皮,把一对儿女装在箩筐里,用扁担担着追赶织女。眼看就要追上时,王母娘娘拔下金簪一划,一条波涛汹涌的天河挡住了牛郎的去路,牛郎和织女被分隔在了天河的两岸。从那以后，牛郎、织女就化作了天上的牛郎星和织女星，隔着天河遥遥相望。后来，王母娘娘允许他们在每年的农历七月七日相见。相传，七月七日这一天，无数喜鹊飞来为他们搭桥，牛郎和织女就在鹊桥上相会。

Niulang (Cowherd) and Zhinü (Weaving Maid from the Heaven) Meet on Magpie Bridge

Niulang and Zhinü are the characters in Chinese mythology. It was said that Niulang's parents passed away when he was just a child, and during the family division, his elder brother and his brother's wife got most of the family property, leaving him only an old ox. Niulang then built a thatched hut on a mountain and lived with the old ox alone. One day, the old ox suddenly opened its mouth to speak and asked Niulang to go to the lake on the other side of the mountain. It said to Niulang that a group of fairies were bathing there and asked him to hide red fairy clothes. Niulang did what the old ox told him and got acquainted with the clothes's owner, namely Zhinü. Later, Niulang and Zhinü got married and gave birth to a son and a daughter. After knowing this, the Queen of Heaven immediately sent the divine troops to arrest Zhinü for violating the heaven rule that a fairy was forbidden to marry a human. With the help of the old ox, Niulang put on the ox leather and carried his children with pole and bamboo baskets to chase Zhinü. When he was about to catch up with Zhinü, the Queen of Heaven took off her gold hairpin and gashed to make a choppy river (the Milky Way) to block him, separating Niulang and Zhinü on the two sides. Since then, Niulang and Zhinü became the Niulang Star (Altair) and the Zhinü Star (Vega) in the sky respectively, which were looking at each other far away from the two sides of the Milky Way. Later, the Queen of Heaven allowed them to meet each other on the seventh day of the seventh lunar month. According to legends, countless magpies would fly to the sky to form a bridge for them to meet each other on that day.

• 绣有"牛郎织女"纹的肚兜（清）

Dudou (Underwear Covering the Chest and Belly) Embroidered with the Pattern of Niulang and Zhinü (Qing Dynasty, 1616-1911)

> 鸟中君子——鸡

鸡是人类最早驯养的动物之一，在距今四千多年前的龙山文化遗址中，就发现了家鸡的骨骼。而殷商时期的文字甲骨文中已经出现了

> Gentleman among Birds: Rooster

Rooster is one of the earliest animals domesticated by humans, and the bones of domestic roosters have been found in Longshan Cultural Ruin, which can be dated back to more than 4,000 years ago. The character "鸡" (*Ji*, meaning rooster) appeared in the oracle bone inscriptions of the Shang Dynasty (1600 B.C.-1046 B.C.), and rooster was mentioned many times in *The Book of Songs* of the Zhou Dynasty (1046 B.C.-256 B.C.). During the Warring States Period (475 B.C.-221 B.C.), many states set up an official position of Rooster Man, who was in charge of sacrifice.

- 四川广汉三星堆遗址出土的青铜鸡
  （图片提供：FOTOE）
  Bronze Rooster Unearthed from Sanxingdui Ruin in Guanghan of Sichuan Province

"鸡"字，周朝的《诗经》里不只一处提到了鸡。战国时期，各国还设有"鸡人"的官职，专司祭祀。

因为公鸡有早晨鸣叫的习性，鸡鸣后日出东方，所以古人认为鸡唤出了太阳。四川广汉三星堆遗址中出土了商代晚期的青铜"金鸡"和"扶桑树"。《神异经》记载："扶桑山有玉鸡，玉鸡鸣则金鸡鸣，金鸡鸣则石鸡鸣，石鸡鸣则天下之鸡悉鸣。"扶桑树是古代传说中的"神树"，鸡飞至桑树的高枝上啼鸣，于是就产生了金鸡鸣叫、日出扶桑的神话。金鸡也成了太阳

Cocks are used to crowing in the morning and the sun rises after the crowing, so the ancients believed that it was the rooster that aroused the sum. Two bronze wares of Golden Rooster and Hibiscus Tree (late Shang Dynasty have been unearthed from the Sanxingdui Ruin in Guanghan of Sichuan Province. According to *Shenyi Jing (Tales of Mystery and Supernatural)*: "There is a jade rooster on the Hibiscus Mountain. If the jade rooster crows, the golden rooster will crow, and then will the stone rooster, and finally all the roosters over the world." Hibiscus tree is a sacred tree in ancient legends. Since roosters fly onto

• 陶鸡（东汉）
Pottery Rooster (Eastern Han Dynasty, 25-220)

• 青釉刻花莲瓣纹鸡首壶（南朝）
Celadon Glazed Rooster-headed Ewer with Carved Lotus Petal Pattern (Southern Dynasties, 420-589)

● 北京颐和园"功名富贵"彩画

牡丹与啼叫的公鸡组成"功名富贵"的吉祥图案。"公"与"功"谐音,"鸣"与"名"谐音,而牡丹为富贵之花,所以公鸡与牡丹组合的"功名富贵"喻示着仕途顺利、富贵、吉祥。

Color Painting of Fame and Fortune in Summer Palace, Beijing
The combination of peony and crowing cock is an auspicious pattern named Fame and Fortune. Since the combination of the Chinese Characters "公" and "鸣" (*Gong and Ming*, meaning a crowing cock) is a homophony of "功名" (*Gongming*, meaning fame), and peony is a flower representing fortune. The pattern combining cock and peony can have the implied meaning of successful official career, fortune and auspiciousness.

的使者和给人间带来光明的"神鸟"。

西汉初期的《韩诗外传》中称赞鸡有"五德":"头戴冠者,文也;足傅距者,武也;敌在前敢斗者,勇也;见食相呼者,仁也;守夜不失时者,信也。""头戴冠者,文也"指的是雄鸡头上有火红的鸡冠,就像戴着一顶漂亮的冠冕,说明鸡是一种彬彬有礼的动物,有着升迁、腾达的寓意。"足

hibiscus trees for crowing, myth is spread that the sun rises from hibiscus trees after the golden rooster's crowing. The golden rooster also becomes the messenger of the sun and the sacred bird that can bring light to human world.

Hanshi Waizhuan (The Tale of Han Ying's Collection of Poetry), written in the early Western Han Dynasty, praises rooster for Five Virtues: "It wears a crown, so educated; it has feet with raised claw toes, so powerful; it dares

● 粉彩花卉雄鸡纹盘（清）
Famille Rose Porcelain Plate with Flowers and Cock Pattern (Qing Dynasty, 1616-1911)

傅距者，武也"，说的是鸡脚后面有突出的形似足趾的"距"，显得威武有力。"敌在前敢斗者，勇也"，说的是鸡面对强敌而不惧，敢于争斗的勇武精神。尤其是带崽的公鸡和母鸡，在雏鸡遇到危险时，会高声尖叫，羽毛倒竖，奋起迎战。"见食相呼者，仁也"，说的是公鸡在觅得食物后会啼叫，呼唤母鸡前来共享，母鸡对自己的子女更是呵护备至。"守夜不失时者，信也"，是说雄鸡天天报晓，是有信义的鸟类。几千年来，鸡伴随着中国人"日出而作，日入而

to fight with enemies ahead, so brave; it calls on partners where there is food, so benevolent; it never misses time for night watching, so faithful." Rooster is educated because it has a red comb on head, which looks like a beautiful crown with a meaning of promotion, proving that rooster is a polite animal. Rooster is powerful because it has raised claw toes on the rear part of its feet, showing that it has a strong power. Rooster is brave because it does not fear strong enemies and has the spirit to fight. Especially when chicks are in danger, the cock and hen will cream loudly and raise their feathers to defeat the enemies. Rooster is benevolent because the cock will call on the hen to share when it finds some food and the hen is very motherly to their children. Rooster is faithful because cock announces the arrival of dawn every day, which proves that rooster is a bird with high trustworthiness. For thousands of years, rooster has been a part of Chinese people's lives when they get up to work at sunrise and have a rest at sunset as it tells time faithfully every day, and thus wins people's praise and love.

As the character "鸡" (*Ji*, meaning rooster) is a homophony of "吉" (*Ji*, meaning auspicious) in Chinese, rooster

- 《芙蓉锦鸡图》 赵佶（宋）

  锦鸡是野鸡的一种，羽毛色彩艳丽，喻示前程似锦、兴旺发达。锦鸡还可与花卉形成"锦上添花"图，喻示好上加好。

  Picture of Lotus and Golden Pheasant, by Zhao Ji (Song Dynasty, 960-1279)

  Golden pheasant is wild rooster, which has colorful feather, meaning a good future and great prosperity. Golden pheasant can also be combined with flowers to form the pattern of Adding Flowers on Golden Pheasant, which has an implied meaning of getting better and better.

息"的生活，每天守信报时，受到人们的赞誉和喜爱。

"鸡"与"吉"谐音，因而鸡自然成了吉祥、幸福的象征。古人认为鸡可以使人远离灾祸，因此过年的时候，人们将鸡的画像贴在门上，旁插桃符，以驱邪迎福。这种风俗一直传承至今，山西大同一带的乡村仍保留着春节在门上贴公鸡剪纸的习俗。

is naturally regarded as a symbol of auspiciousness and happiness. The ancients believed that rooster could keep themselves away from disasters. So during the Chinese New Year, people would post rooster pictures on the doors and inserted peach branches next to them, so as to ward off evils and welcome bliss. This custom has been passed down until present day. Villages in Datong of Shanxi Province, for instance, still keep the custom of posting cock paper-cuts on doors during the Spring Festival.

> 安居乐业——鹌鹑

鹌鹑是一种古老的鸟类，分布极广，品种繁多。中国是鹌鹑的主要产地之一，也是饲养鹌鹑最早的国家之一。《诗经》中有"不狩不猎，胡瞻尔庭有县鹑兮"的诗句。

中国人早期驯养鹌鹑不是为了食用，而是为了玩乐。鹌鹑还有吉

> Stable Settle-down and Content Job: Quail

Quail is a kind of ancient bird, which is widespread with assorted varieties. China is one of the main producing areas for quails and is also one of the earliest countries to raise quails. In *The Book of Songs*, there is a verse saying: "you did not go hurting, but why I see there are quails hunting in your house?"

In early stage, Chinese people's purpose of domesticating quails was not for eating, but for entertainment. In addition to fighting, quail is also used

- 《鹌鹑图页》（宋）
  Quail Drawing Sheet (Song Dynasty, 960-1279)

- 鹌鹑形玉盒（清）
  Quail-shaped Jade Box (Qing Dynasty, 1616-1911)

- "安居乐业"图瓶（清）

  鹌鹑的"鹌"与"安"谐音，菊花的"菊"与"居"谐音，组合在一起就成了"安居乐业"。

  Bottle with Pattern of Stable Settle-down and Content Job

  The character "鹌" (*An*, meaning quail) is a homophony of "安" (*An*, meaning stable) and "菊" (*Ju*, meaning chrysanthemum) is a homophony of "居" (*Ju*, meaning settle-down), thus the combination of quail and chrysanthemum has the meaning of Stable Settle-down and Content Job.

祥的寓意。鹌鹑雌鸟与雄鸟有固定的配偶，常见两只鹌鹑形影不离，而且"鹌"与"安"谐音，所以人们把鹌鹑作为爱情和谐、生活安定的象征。

to imply auspiciousness. As quail is monogamy bird that always appears in pair, and as "鹌" (*An*, meaning quail) is a homophony of "安" (*An*, meaning stable), so quail is seen as a symbol of harmonious love and stable life.

> 夫妻偕老——白头翁

白头翁鸟学名为"白头鹎",是一种鹎科的小型鸟类,最大的特点是头顶有一圈白色的绒毛。这种鸟在中国长江以南的广大地区十分常见,多活动于丘陵或平原的灌木丛中,生性活泼,十分可爱。

白头翁头上一圈白色的羽毛,就像长寿的老人的白发,所以从古

> Live to Old Age in Conjugal Bliss: Chinese Bulbul

Chinese bulbul's scientific name is Pycnonotus sinensis, which is a kind of small grackle bird with a feature that there is a ring of white fluff on the head. This kind of lively and lovely bird is very common in the vast area south to the Yangtze River in China and mostly inhabits in thickets among hills or plains.

As the white fluff on Chinese

- 《杂画册之萱草白头翁》 朱耷（清）
  Album of Paintings: Hemerocallis Fulva and Chinese Bulbul, by Zhu Da (Qing Dynasty, 1616-1911)

- 北京颐和园长廊中的"富贵白头"彩画

  白头翁与牡丹花组成"白头富贵"的图案。牡丹是富贵、吉祥的象征,"白头富贵"有夫妻白头偕老、富贵、美满的寓意。

  Color Painting of White Hair and Fortune on the Long Corridor in Summer Palace, Beijing

  The pattern of White Hair and Fortune is formed by Chinese bulbul and peony. As peony is a symbol of fortune and auspiciousness, the pattern can mean that a couple will live to old age in conjugal bliss, and have a perfect life with great fortune.

至今,白头翁一直被中国人看作长寿的象征。而且白头翁有固定的伴侣,经常双宿、双飞,所以也常常被用来喻示夫妻恩爱,白头偕老。

bulbul's head looks like the white hair of long-lived seniors, the Chinese bulbul has been seen as a symbol of longevity since ancient times. What's more, Chinese bulbul has a fixed spouse and often appears in pair, so it is also used to imply an affectionate couple living to old age in conjugal bliss.

> 长寿富贵——绶带鸟

　　绶带鸟又名"寿带鸟""练鹊""白带子"等，主要分布在中国的东部和中部地区，体形与麻雀相似。此鸟头部的羽毛为带有金属光泽的蓝黑色，头顶有一簇冠羽，鸣叫时可耸起。最特别的是，雄性绶带鸟有两根长长的尾羽，可达身

> Longevity and Fortune: Paradise Flycatcher

Paradise flycatcher, also known as *Shoudai Niao*, *Lianjuan* or *Baidaizi*, is mainly distributed in China's eastern and central regions and its body is similar to that of the sparrow. The feather on its head is in blue-black color with metallic luster, and the crest hair on its head can rise up when it tweets. The most special is that male paradise flycatcher has two long tail quills on its rear, which can be two or three times the length of its body and will flutter with the wind when it is flying, so beautiful that it has won a lot of love from people since ancient times. As recorded in *Compendium of Materia Medica* written by Li Shizhen in the

- 碧玉绶带鸟摆件（清）
  Jasper Decorations in the Shape of Paradise Flycatcher (Qing Dynasty, 1616-1911)

● 北京北海公园琼岛延楼长廊上的"富贵长寿"彩画

绶带鸟与牡丹花组合成"富贵长寿"的吉祥含义。绶带鸟象征吉祥，牡丹花代表富贵，二者结合表达了人们追求富贵、长寿、生活幸福的愿望。

Color Painting of Fortune and Longevity on the Long Corridor of Yanlou Building on Jade Islet in Beihai Park, Beijing

The combination of paradise flycatcher and peony has the auspicious meaning of fortune and longevity. Paradise flycatcher symbolizes auspiciousness and represents fortune, thus their combination expresses people's desire to pursue fortune, longevity and happy lives.

长的两三倍，飞翔时随风飘动，十分美丽，自古就受到人们的喜爱。明代医学家李时珍撰写的《本草纲目》中记载："练鹊，其尾长，白毛如练带者是也。""绶带"是一种以丝线织成的带子，在古代是公侯或官员身份的代表，以此为名的绶带鸟因而也具有了高贵、荣耀的象征意义。此外，因"绶"与"寿"谐音，所以绶带鸟也具有长寿、富贵的吉祥含义。

Ming Dynasty (1368-1644), "*Lianjuan* has a long tail and its white feather looks like sashes." And *Shoudai* refers to a kind of ribbon made of silk threads and used to represent the status of nobles and officials in ancients, thus *Shoudai Niao*, which is named after *Shoudai*, has a symbolic meaning of fortune and glory. In addition, as the character "绶" (*Shou*, meaning paradise flycatcher) is a homophony of "寿" (*Shou*, meaning longevity), paradise flycatcher also has an auspicious meaning of longevity and fortune.

"举案齐眉"的由来

《后汉书·梁鸿传》中记载，东汉初的著名学者梁鸿品德高尚，许多有权势的人家都想把女儿嫁给他，却都被他拒绝了。与他同县的女子孟氏，长得又黑又丑，力气极大，三十岁了还没有出嫁，发誓非梁鸿不嫁。梁鸿听说后，就下聘礼娶了孟氏。经过一段时间的相处，梁鸿认为孟氏勤俭持家，是自己的贤德之妻，因此为她取名为孟光，字德耀，喻示她的仁德像光芒一样闪耀。后来，他们二人隐居山林之中，每次梁鸿外出回家，孟光都会把饭菜做好，并放在食案上，然后把食案举到与眉毛相齐的位置递给梁鸿，表示对他的尊敬。后来人们就用"举案齐眉"形容夫妻相互尊敬、恩爱、幸福。

Origin of *Ju'an Qimei* (Hold up the Tray as High as Eyebrows)

According to the *Book of the Later Han Dynasty: Biography of Liang Hong*, there was a famous scholar named Liang Hong in the early Eastern Han Dynasty, who had noble morality, and many influential people wanted to marry their daughters to him, but he refused all of them. In the county Liang Hong lived, there was a Miss Meng, who was black, ugly, strong, and still unmarried at the age of 30. What's more, she vowed that she would not marry anyone except Liang Hong. Hearing about this, Liang Hong presented a dowry to Miss Meng's family and married her. Getting along with each other for a period of time, Liang Hong found that his wife was frugal and virtuous, so he gave her a formal name of Meng Guang (*Meng* is the family name and *Guang* means lights) and a courtesy name of Deyao (*De* means virtue, and *Yao* means shine), meaning that his wife's virtue was shining like lights. Later, the couple withdrew from society and lived in mountain areas, and every time when Liang Hong came back, Meng Guang would place the food she had made on a tray, and then would hold the tray up to the position as high as her eyebrows to present food for her husband, so as to show her respect. From that on, people began to use the idiom of *Ju'an Qimei* (hold up the tray as high as eyebrows) to describe a married couple who love and respect each other for life.

• 《梅花绶带图》 沈铨（清）
Painting of Plum Blossom and Paradise Flycatcher, by Shen Quan (Qing Dynasty, 1616-1911)

> 优雅自由——鹭鸶

鹭鸶又称"白鹭",在中国古代也称"丝禽",属于鹭科的一种水鸟。它们浑身洁白,体态修长,繁殖期间,头上会生出两根十几厘米长的羽毛,胸背处也会长出丝状的长羽毛,随着自身的起舞而飘动,十分美丽。白鹭的生活地域很广,喜欢栖息在湖泊、沼泽地和潮湿的森林里,靠灵活的脖子和鱼叉

> Elegance and Freedom: Egret

Egret, also known as White Egret or *Siqin* (filamentous bird) in ancient China, is an *Ardeidae* water bird. Its slender body is in full white, and during the breeding period, its head will send up two 10 cm long plumes while its chest and back will also outgrow filamentous long feathers, which will flutter beautifully when dancing. With a wide-range distribution, egret likes to perch on lakes, swamps or in humid woods. With a flexible neck and a fishing-fork-like sharp mouth, it is good at foraging food in shallow water, which mainly includes small fishes, reptiles, amphibians and crustaceans living in

- 荷花鹭鸶纹盒(清)
  Box with Pattern of Lotus and Egrets (Qing Dynasty, 1616-1911)

● 山西太原晋祠的"一路连科"彩画
Color Painting of Continuous Successes in All Exams at Jinci Temple in Taiyuan, Shanxi Province

一样的尖嘴在浅水中觅食，主要以小型鱼类、爬行动物、两栖动物和浅水中的甲壳类动物为食。休息的时候，白鹭经常缩起一只脚，单腿立在水中，姿态非常优美。

白鹭自古就深受人们喜爱。唐代诗人杜甫就有"两个黄鹂鸣翠柳，一行白鹭上青天"的名句，描绘出了众多白鹭飞上天际的井然有序的美景。唐代另一位诗人张志和在其名作《渔歌子》中写道："西塞山前白鹭飞，桃花流水鳜鱼肥。

shallow water. During the resting time, egret often shrinks up a foot and stands on one leg in the water, making a very beautiful posture.

Egret has been liked since ancient times. Du Fu, a poet of the Tang Dynasty once wrote a famous verse: "Two orioles are tweeting on green willow, and a line of egrets are flying into the sky." It depicts a beautiful scenery that numerous egrets are flying into the sky in a well-regulated order. Zhang Zhihe, another poet of the Tang Dynasty, also wrote

青箬笠，绿蓑衣，斜风细雨不须归。"大意是，白鹭在西塞山前自由地翱翔，肥美的鳜鱼在漂着桃花的江水中欢快地游动。江边的渔翁戴着青色的箬笠，披着绿色的蓑衣，在斜风细雨中垂钓，悠然自得，并不急着回家。白鹭成为传统文化和人们心目中高贵、优雅、纯洁、自由的象征。

鹭鸶可与莲花、芦苇组成"一路连科"图案，其中，"鹭"与"路"

in his famous poem *Yugezi*: "Egrets are flying freely in front of Xisai Mountain, while fat mandarin fishes are swimming joyfully in running water with peach blossoms floating on. By the river, a fisherman, wearing a bamboo-leaf hat and a green coir raincoat, is fishing in slanting wind and drizzling rain leisurely and contently, and is not in a hurry to go home." Egret is seen as a symbol of dignity, elegance, purity and freedom in traditional culture and people's minds.

The combination of egrets, lotus and reeds can form the pattern of *Yilu Lianke* (continuous successes in all exams, *Yilu* means continuous and *Lianke* means successes in all exams) because the character "鹭" (*Lu*, meaning egret) is a homophone of "路" (*Lu*, one character of the compound word *Yiyu*), the character "莲" (*Lian*, meaning lotus) is a homophone of "连" (*Lian*, one character of the compound word *Lianke*),

- 青白玉鹭鸶衔莲荷叶形卣（清）
Greenish-white Jade Wine Vessel with Carving of Egret Holding Lotus Leaves in Mouth (Qing Dynasty, 1616-1911)

- 黑缎地绣"一路连科"纹暖耳（清）
  暖耳又称"耳套"，是古人在冬季套在耳朵上的一种保暖装饰。
  Black Satin Ear Warmer with Embroidered Pattern of Continuous Successes in All Exams (Qing Dynasty, 1616-1911)
  Ear warmer, also known as earmuff, is kind of warm decoration wore on ears by the ancients in winter.

谐音，"莲"与"连"谐音，而芦苇棵棵相连，取"棵"与"科"谐音。

"一路连科"的寓意是考生在古代科举的各级考试中连得头名，连科高中，顺利进入仕途。

and the character "棵" (*Ke*, meaning the connecting reeds) is a homophone of "科" (*Ke*, another character of the compound word *Lianke*). The pattern's implied meaning is to wish students continuous successes in different levels of ancient imperial examinations and hope them to obtain an official career smoothly.

> 仁德守信——大雁

大雁是雁属鸟类的通称，在中国常见的有白额雁、鸿雁、豆雁、斑头雁、灰雁等几种，它们共同的特点是体型较大，颈部粗而短，翅膀长而尖，体羽大多为褐色、灰色或白色。

大雁是一种集群的候鸟，自古以来就为人们所熟知。在迁徙时，雁群总是几十只、数百只集中在一起列队而飞，古人称之为"雁

> Kindness and Trustworthing: Wild Goose

Wild goose is the collective name of anser birds and the breeds commonly seen in China include white-fronted goose, swan goose, bean goose, bar-headed goose, grey goose, etc., which share common features of big body, thick and short neck, long and pointed wings, and feathers mainly in brown, gray or white colors.

Wild goose is a kind of gregarious migratory bird, which has been well known by people since ancient times. During the migration, dozens or hundreds of wild geese always fly together in lines, which were called Goose Queue

- 芦雁图瓷虎枕（金）
  Tiger-shaped Porcelain Pillow with Pattern of Reeds and Wild Geese (Jin Dynasty, 1115-1234)

• 彩绘雁鱼铜灯（西汉）
Painted Bronze Lamp in Shape of Wild Goose and Fish (Western Han Dynasty, 206 B.C.-25 A.D.)

阵"。在有经验的"头雁"的带领下，大雁的队伍排成"人"字形或"一"字形，并且经常变换队形，更换"头雁"。雁群的迁徙大多在黄昏或夜晚进行，在旅途中会选择湖泊水域休息和进食。雁群每一次迁徙都要耗费一两个月的时间，历尽千辛万苦，但它们每年春天北往，秋天南来，从不失信。

by the ancients. With the guide of an experienced leading goose, the wild geese usually line up in the form of " 人 " (*Ren*, meaning person) or " 一 " (*Yi*, meaning one), and often change their formation and the leading goose. Most of the wild geese migrate in the evening or at night and choose lake waters for resting and feeding during the journey. It takes wild geese one or two months to finish a migration, which is an arduous journey full of dangers and hardships. In spite of that, wild geese still move to the north in spring and come back to the south in autumn every year, with no exception.

Since long-distance transport was very inconvenient in ancient times, the wanderers far away from home would often feel homesick and sad about staying in strange place when they saw wild geese, which travel between the north and the south every year. For example, Xue Daoheng, a poet of the Sui Dynasty wrote a famous verse in his poem *Renri Sigui*: "Early before the flowers came into blossom, I got the idea to go home; however, the wild geese are flying back to the north, but I am still here."

There have been folk legends about swan geese for communication in China since ancient times when means

由于大雁每年南来北往，在长途交通极为不便的古代，远方的游子看到雁群，常常会引发思乡之情和羁旅的伤感。如隋代诗人薛道衡《人日思归》的名句"人归落雁后，思发在花前"就表达了这种情感。

• 《芦雁图轴》 朱耷（清）
Scroll Painting of Reeds and Wild Geese, by Zhu Da (Qing Dynasty, 1616-1911)

of communication were limited and people wanted to use such punctual and trustworthy migratory birds to deliver messages and information. According to *The Records of History*, in 100 B.C. (1st year of the Period of Tianhan during the reign of Emperor Wu of the Western Han Dynasty), the imperial corps commander Su Wu was missioned to Huns and then was detained in the bitter cold region of the Beihai (present Lake Baikal) for 18 years. Later, the Han-dynasty government sent an ambassador to require the Huns to release Su Wu, but the chief of Huns lied to the ambassador that Su Wu had been dead. Chang Hui, a man who came with Su Wu 18 years ago, told the ambassador secretly that Su Wu was still alive. The ambassador then said to the chief of Huns that the emperor of the Han Dynasty had shot a swan goose during hunting, and on the foot of it, he had found a silk manuscript, saying that Su Wu was still alive. As a result, the Huns realized that they could not hide the truth anymore and had to release Su Wu. This story later became a classical anecdote while wild goose became the synonym of messenger.

The ancients believed that wild goose was a sacred bird possessing the Five Constant Virtues, which

• 寿山石芦雁图薄意章料
Shoushan Stone Seal Material Carved with Pattern of Reeds and Wild Geese

中国民间自古就有"鸿雁传书"的传说，因为古人的通信手段有限，希望通过这种守时而有信的候鸟来传递书信和信息。据《史记》记载，汉武帝天汉元年（前100年），中郎将苏武出使匈奴，被拘留并关押在北海（今贝加尔湖）的苦寒地区18年。后来，汉朝派使者前往，要求匈奴释放苏武，匈奴单于却谎称苏武已死。与苏武一同出使的常惠秘密见到汉使，说苏武没有死。于是使者对单于说：汉天子在打猎时射到一只鸿雁，雁足上系着一块帛书，上面说苏武尚在人世。这样一来，匈奴无法隐瞒，只得把苏武放归汉朝。这个故事成为千古佳话，鸿雁也就成了"信使"的代称。

古人认为大雁是具有"五常"的"灵禽"，"五常"指古代儒家所推崇的"仁、义、礼、智、信"五种德行。在一个雁群中，年老、病弱的大雁飞行较慢，其余强壮的同伴却不会弃之不顾，此为仁者之

referred to the Confucian advocating of benevolence, loyalty, propriety, wisdom and trustworthiness in ancient times. Wild goose's benevolence lies in that the strong geese will not abandon the the elderly, sick or weak when they fly too slowly. Wild geese are loyal because the male and female ones are faithful to each other until death. Wild goose's propriety lies in that the goose queues always fly in lines with a well-regulated order during the migration and the young and strong ones will never surpass the old leading one ahead. Wild goose's

蝴蝶

蝴蝶是一种美丽的昆虫，被誉为"会飞的花朵"。在中国传统文化中，蝴蝶是高雅、华贵的代表。同时，由于蝴蝶经常成双、成对地在花间飞舞，也成为幸福、爱情的象征。蝴蝶图案常以两只蝴蝶或蝴蝶与别的花草、禽鸟组合的形式构成，比较常见的有"蝶恋花""猫蝶富贵""瓜瓞绵绵"等几种。

Butterfly

The butterfly is a beautiful insect, which is honored as Flying Flower and is seen as a representation of elegance and luxuriousness in traditional Chinese culture. Meanwhile, as butterflies often fly in pairs among flowers, they are also regarded as a symbol of happiness and love. Butterfly pattern usually consists of two butterflies or a butterfly combined with other flowers or birds, and the most common ones include Butterfly Loving Flower, Cat and Butterfly with Fortune, *Guadie Mianmian* (melons and butterflies, implying an endless inheritance for a family), and so on.

- 黄缎蝶恋花图案女氅衣（清）
Yellow Satin Woman Cloak with Pattern of Butterfly Loving Flower (Qing Dynasty, 1616-1911)

• 粉彩芦雁图茶壶
Famille Rose Porcelain Tea Pot with Pattern of Reeds and Wild Geese

心。大雁一雌、一雄两两相配，从一而终，这是有情、有义的表现。迁徙中的大雁飞行时排成队列，整齐而有序，其中青壮年大雁不会越到带头的老雁之前，这是谦恭、有礼的表现。无论是飞行还是落地歇息，雁群中都会有壮雁负责警戒，十分敏锐、机警，体现了大雁的智慧。大雁定期迁徙，是坚毅、守信的表现。"五常"俱全的大雁成为最受中国人喜爱和尊敬的禽鸟之一。

wisdom lies in that it is the strong ones that always take the responsibility of safeguarding whether they are flying in sky or resting on ground. In addition, wild geese are trustworthy because they keep migrating in a regular time. In a word, wild goose, which possesses the Five Constant Virtues, has become one of the most loved and respectable birds for the Chinese people.